42

THE BUDGERIGAR BOOK

THE
BUDGERIGAR
BOOK

by

ERNEST HOWSON

assisted by specialist contributors

Published by:
SAIGA PUBLISHING CO. LTD.
1 Royal Parade, Hindhead, Surrey
GU26 6TD ENGLAND

ISBN 0 904558 85 1

Typesetting by
Ebony Typesetting, Nr. Liskeard, Cornwall

Published by:
SAIGA PUBLISHING CO. LTD.
1 Royal Parade, Hindhead, Surrey
GU26 6TD England

CONTENTS

MONOCHROME ILLUSTRATIONS LIST

COLOURED ILLUSTRATIONS LIST

ACKNOWLEDGEMENTS

In this book, I have attempted to bring together all of those matters affecting the production of good exhibition Budgerigars. During the past 20 years, many people, perhaps unknown to themselves, have helped in the writing of this book; Syd Ambler, who taught me my first steps in genetics and Chris Harrington who helped me with that subject; the late Dr H. J. O'Loughlin, who taught me about metabolism, not to mention the many breeders with whom I have come into contact over the years who taught me that Budgerigar breeding is not always a matter of what can or cannot be written down. Ray Brown of York especially, for his help in the writing of this book, and not least, **The Budgerigar Society** for its kind permission in the reproduction of the *standards*.

The publishers would like to thank the following who kindly supplied photographs; Ponderosa of Cheltenham; Cage and Aviary Birds; and Ivy Cottage Bird Farm, Shedfield.

Figure 1.1   Budgerigars in the Wild

CHAPTER 1

THE HISTORY OF THE EXHIBITION BUDGERIGAR

The Budgerigar (*Melopsittacus undulatus*) is a bird of Australian origin which was first brought to England in 1840 by John Gould, and quickly became so popular that those fortunate enough to have acquired breeding pairs were soon keeping them in very large numbers.

The first imported birds were the wild Light Greens, but eventually, over the years, colour mutations developed which breeders, by judicious selection, paired to one another until the colours became commonplace. Such mutations commanded very high prices when they were first evolved but, as they became more common, their prices dropped again, until the next mutation appeared.

In the wild, the Budgerigar, which is sometimes referred to as the Australian Grass Parakeet* is a gregarious creature, living in large flocks and feeding from seeding grasses, not to mention cereal crops, which can make it something of a nuisance to the Australian arable farmer.

The name of the bird comes from the Aboriginal 'betcherrygah', which, translated literally, means good food. Surely a pointer to the use of the bird from the point of view of the Aborigines! In the wild, the Budgerigar nests in dead trees, hence the provision of nest boxes by breeders, simulating those conditions.

The wild birds bear little relation, visually, to the exhibition birds of today, and the exhibition Budgerigar can be fairly said to have been

*Also known as: *Warbling Grass Parakeet*, *Zebra Parakeet*, *Psittacus undulatus*, *Undulated Parrot*, *Euphema undulatus*, *Nanondes undulatus*, *Canary Parrot*, *Betcherrygah* and *Scolloped Parakeet*.

evolved by man. If one looks at the earliest drawings of the standard exhibition bird and compares these with the present *standards*, the differences are perfectly clear; only by careful selection of breeding partners have fanciers been able to change the size and shape of the exhibition specimen.

In the early days of the Fancy, from perhaps 1885 to around 1930, when the different colour varieties were evolving, very high prices were paid for birds because of their, then, unusual colours rather than as is the case today when a bird would have to be a good overall exhibition specimen to command a high price, regardless of its colour.

It is probably also true to say that apart from the interest shown in it by aviculturalists in the early days, the Budgerigar as an exhibition bird owes much of its popularity to the fact that it is the most popular pet bird, and is kept in many thousands of living rooms throughout the world.

The constant chatter and amusing antics of the pet Budgerigar make it enjoyable as a companion for young and old alike, and this gives an added incentive to the breeder, and has also unquestionably played a large part in the development of the exhibition bird. A breeder of Budgerigars, who wishes to keep only those specimens which will produce first class young, will perhaps obtain only one bird per season from any given pair which he wishes to keep for the purposes of perpetuating the line and the quality of his stud. Because of the popularity of the Budgerigar, however, he will have little if any difficulty in disposing of his unwanted stock, and, at the same time, will make at least a little money which will help to pay for the development of his exhibition birds.

This situation has been the case through almost the entire history of the Budgerigar, exhibition or otherwise, since its introduction to this country, and the same almost certainly applies to other countries of the world. Indeed, such is known to be the case in France and Belgium, where the Budgerigar enjoyed possibly even greater popularity than in this country.

The very first exhibition birds are believed to have been shown in the early 1920's, but since then, and with the growth of serious breeding as a hobby, shows now attract hundreds of birds, especially the larger shows, as for example **The Budgerigar Society's** Annual Show, where birds of every colour and type can be seen to their best advantage.

Since the mid-1950's, the fancy as a whole which grew rapidly during those years, has declined a little, but it is still the most popular of all species. Its nearest challenger, the Border Canary, comes nowhere near, relatively speaking, the popularity of the Budgerigar.

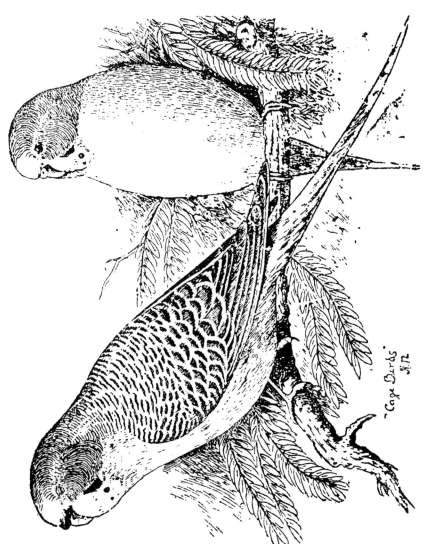

Figure 1.2   An Early Drawing of Domestic Budgerigars

It is my belief that in future years, the popularity of the bird will continue to grow as the working week becomes shorter, as it inevitably will, and people look for some outlet to occupy their free time.

SPECIAL NOTE

Readers wishing to study the history of the domesticated Budgerigar are referred to the fascinating study by Cyril H. Rogers — *The World of Budgerigars* (Saiga).

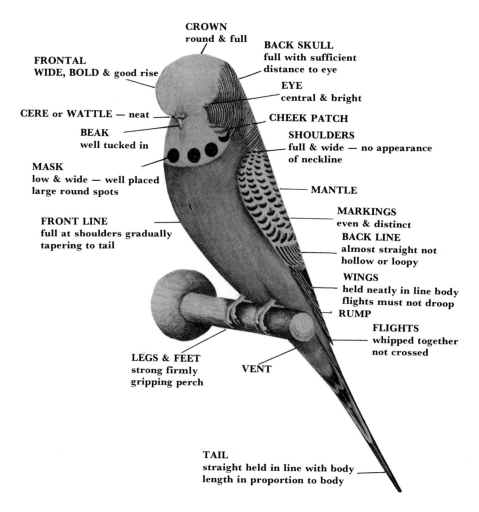

CROWN
round & full

BACK SKULL
full with sufficient
distance to eye

FRONTAL
WIDE, BOLD & good rise

EYE
central & bright

CERE or WATTLE — neat

CHEEK PATCH

BEAK
well tucked in

SHOULDERS
full & wide — no appearance
of neckline

MASK
low & wide — well placed
large round spots

MANTLE

MARKINGS
even & distinct

FRONT LINE
full at shoulders gradually
tapering to tail

BACK LINE
almost straight not
hollow or loopy

WINGS
held neatly in line body
flights must not droop

RUMP

FLIGHTS
whipped together
not crossed

LEGS & FEET
strong firmly
gripping perch

VENT

TAIL
straight held in line with body
length in proportion to body

Figure 1.3 Main Features of the *Standard* Budgerigar (*Courtesy:* The Budgerigar Society)

4

CHAPTER 2

BUILDING THE AVIARY

BIRD ROOM VITAL TO SUCCESS

The ultimate aim of all breeders of exhibition Budgerigars, is success on the show bench. The consistent achievement of that aim depends upon a logical progression of factors in the same way that each successive link in a chain is dependent upon the link preceding it. If the preceding link is broken, then the remainder of the chain will fail and become useless for the purpose for which it was intended. If that analogy is applied to the breeding of Budgerigars, then the first link in the chain must be the most fundamental of all, the bird room, and the conditions under which the stock will be expected to live, and perhaps more importantly for the breeder of exhibition stock, to produce young of high quality. Unless the stock is housed in comfortable surroundings, success in terms of breeding, or for that matter keeping the existing stock in good physical condition, will certainly be more difficult than if they are housed in unsuitable conditions. Before considering the birds, therefore, it is essential that a careful study should be made of the size, type and ancillary equipment of the bird room before any thought is given to the actual acquisition of stock or its management.

MATERIALS

Building with Brick

The first decision which must be made before work on building the bird room can begin, is to choose which materials are to be used in its construction.

There is no doubt that the best material for the purpose is brick, and if the fancier's finances will allow, then there is no argument. A brick built bird room is much easier to keep at an even temperature, and that

5

Figure 2.1   A Large Modern Bird Room: note the outside flights at each end, and the louvred glass windows

applies to summer and winter alike; it requires far less maintenance than a wooden structure, and, of course, it will last much longer. The main arguments against the erection of a brick built bird room, are its cost, and the time it takes to build, but there is another point which should be considered.

Large numbers enter the Budgerigar fancy every year by setting up a stud of birds. Unfortunately for the fancy in general, many leave the ranks of Budgerigar fanciers after perhaps only three or four seasons. Because of that fact, the beginner would be perhaps better advised to start with a more modest structure, even if he is able to afford to erect a brick building, and to make sure that his interest will be kept up, before going to the expense of erecting a large and costly bird room.

Building with timber

Apart from brick, the next best material, and that which is by far the most widely used in building Budgerigar bird rooms, is ship lap timber. This type of building material is durable and efficient, and if it is well maintained, will be perfectly adequate for the purpose.

Plywood is not recommended, even though the use of this type of material makes building much easier. Building experts have advised that, although plywood manufactured for exterior use is reasonably durable, such material will be far less durable than ship lap. The problem, apparently, is that sooner or later dampness will begin to seep into the cut ends of the ply board, resulting in the layers separating. When this happens, the only remedy is the replacement of the entire board. This, depending upon the situation of the particular board in relation to the structure of the building as a whole, may possibly result in almost the entire demolition and rebuilding of the bird room.

Tongued and grooved boards could be used, but this type of timber is more prone to open up at the joints between the boards than is ship lap. If that should happen, then replacement of a single board would be difficult if damage to the adjacent boards is to be avoided. If, however, tongued and grooved board is to be the material used, then it is essential to make very sure that there are no minute gaps between one board and the next. If such gaps do exist, then water will certainly enter, eventually rotting the timber. In my view, the only reason for the use of tongued and grooved boarding in preference to ship lap would be on economic grounds, if the individual fancier was able to obtain sufficient materials very cheaply. Because of the points mentioned in discussing the different types of timber, I have no hesitation in recommending the ship lap type.

READY MADE AVIARIES

Many fanciers who are not 'do it yourself' experts will prefer to buy an

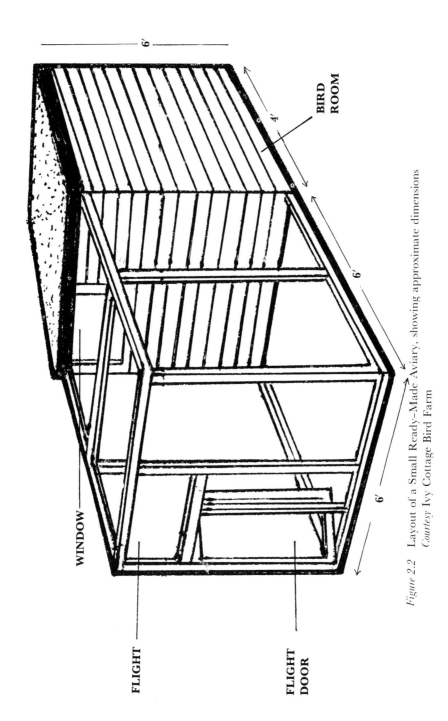

6'

BIRD ROOM

4'

6'

6'

WINDOW

FLIGHT

FLIGHT DOOR

Figure 2.2 Layout of a Small Ready-Made Aviary, showing approximate dimensions
Courtesy Ivy Cottage Bird Farm

aviary from a specialised dealer. These aviaries come in a variety of sizes and may be purchased with or without an outside flight. Generally such aviaries are quite easy to erect and so the fancier with very little time on his hands will find that he can obtain an aviary and birds and be all ready to go within, say, seven days.

If he becomes established in a substantial way, he can then consider having a brick building built which is obviously the ideal. Names and addresses of suppliers of wooden buildings may be found in the advertisements in *Cage and Aviary Birds.*

Metal and Asbestos

Under no circumstances should corrugated metal sheets or asbestos sheets be used. Such materials will result in the building becoming overheated in summer, and too cold in winter. Since the maintenance of an even temperature is important, as we shall see later, this type of building material is best avoided. Similar remarks apply to corrugated perspex sheets. Beginners have on occasion asked whether a bird room constructed of this material would be suitable, especially, I suspect, because it is relatively cheap and easy to use. The answer to the question, is a very definite 'no', for reasons similar to those applying to the use of metal sheets. For the same reasons, it is not practical to convert a greenhouse into a bird room, another question which is frequently asked by beginners.

PREPARING THE SITE

Having decided upon what materials should be used, the next logical progression is to decide upon the site of the bird room. The most advantageous site is one which will allow the bird room to face south or south east. With the bird room in such a position, the interior will derive the benefit of more sunlight during the breeding season than would be the case if the room faced any other direction. Opinions differ within the fancy on this question. The general opinion most widely held, however, states that the position of the bird room has a direct bearing on breeding results. Other fanciers, who have for one reason or another been forced to move their bird rooms from having a southerly aspect, appear to be of the opinion that undesirable as such a move is said to be, breeding results have been equally good, and in some cases, even better. It would be true to say, however, that the former opinion is that most widely held, and my belief is that it is the correct opinion, although not for the reasons most popularly held.

In my view, the advantage of having the bird room facing south, is that the young birds will unquestionably benefit from the extra sunlight.

9

All living things, animal or vegetable, need the benefits of natural sunlight in order to grow and prosper from a point of view of health, and I believe that young Budgerigars are no exception. For that reason alone, I would, wherever it is possible, recommend a southerly aspect. Only if it is absolutely unavoidable should the bird room be placed facing north. A bird room placed in such a position will obviously receive far less natural sunlight, and another disadvantage is that especially in winter, temperatures will be very difficult to control. This is not to say that it is impossible to breed Budgerigars in northerly facing bird rooms. A bird room so placed, however, does, as we have seen, have certain disadvantages.

PLANNING PERMISSION

There are other factors which must be considered when the site of the bird room is being selected. Depending upon the size, shape, position and proximity to one's neighbours, of both garden and bird room, there may be local government laws which would prevent the erection of the room on the desired site. On the other hand, it may be that the erection of the bird room comes within what is termed 'permitted development'. If that is the case, then so much the better, but if it is not, then permission will have to be obtained from the local council planning office. I strongly advise the fancier who is thinking of erecting a bird room to visit his local planning office and to find out very precisely what he can and cannot do in this respect. Indeed, I would go so far as to say that such an exercise is not only necessary, but essential before building is begun.

EXTERNAL DISTRACTIONS

It is almost certain that unless the fancier has a very large garden, he will be unable to site the bird room in such a manner as to shield all possible sources of external distraction. What he must do, however, is to try to place the bird room in such a position that these are kept to an absolute minimum.

Street lights can be a great nuisance, and the bird room should not be placed in such a position that light from this source is able to enter it.

Avoid, if possible, having the windows facing on to a fence. The tops of fences provide excellent vantage points for cats, which will, if not prevented, spend hours sitting on them, watching the birds, and more importantly, disturbing them.

Budgerigars are by no means as timid or as easily frightened as are canaries or foreign birds, but it is better not to tempt fate, especially in the breeding season. If the bird room can be sited in such a manner that the birds are unable to see, for example, children playing in neighbouring gardens or similar distractions, then so much the better. Under normal circumstances, such matters would disturb the birds very little if at all, but in the breeding season the hens may not take kindly to such things.

One possible source of external disturbance which should be given attention, is the possibility of the headlights of passing cars shining into the room. This situation should certainly be avoided, as also should the possibility of light entering the bird room at night from the house.

Avoiding the external influences may be difficult, but if they can be overcome with a little forethought, then the time spent in solving the problems will unquestionably have been well spent.

LAYING THE BASE

Having finally decided upon the site of the bird room, the direction which it is to face, and having ascertained that its erection in that position is acceptable to the local authority and to one's neighbours, a decision must be made on whether a concrete base should be laid. I believe that most fanciers would agree that although a concrete base is certainly not essential, it is very desirable.

Such a base has a number of advantages. It gives the bird room, which with its cages and equipment installed will be quite heavy, a firm foundation upon which to stand, thus avoiding the possibility of one part or another sinking and leaving an uneven floor. It is a great help in keeping out vermin, and perhaps most important of all, it will keep the supporting beams away from the damp ground and will prevent damp rot from setting in. Such a base will also prevent rising damp, and for all these reasons, its cost is justified.

When a concrete base is being installed, it is important to remember that the cavity into which the rubble is placed, beneath the concrete surface, should be lined with polythene or some other rot proof material. This will prevent the base itself from becoming damp, and, consequently, the bird room.

SIZE

The dimensions of a Budgerigar breeding room are not in themselves important from a purely breeding point of view. What is important, however, is that the bird room should be sufficiently large for the number of birds which will be living in it, and that there is sufficient space left over when the breeding pairs are occupying their quarters to accommodate the offspring which will be produced.

It would not be advisable to make a start with a bird room measuring less than 10 feet (3 m) by 8 feet (2.44 m) for that reason. The height is, of course, variable, but since Budgerigar breeding cages are installed in tiers, the fancier setting up a bird room should bear in mind that an extra 6 inches (15 cm) in the height of the room may result in his being able to install another tier of cages along the full length, and in terms of a smaller sized room, this may be a very important point.

It would also, perhaps, be a little unfair to advise the beginner in particular to start with a larger structure, which would certainly be expensive. If, as we have previously discussed, the fancier loses his interest in Budgerigars, then he may well have to face a large capital loss. If, however, he begins with a bird room of modest but adequate size, then such a bird room will be reasonably easily disposed of if the fancier then wishes to expand his interest, and probably at relatively small cost, especially if the structure has been well maintained.

PLANNING THE BIRD ROOM

One of the most important aspects of the setting up of a bird room is the planning stage. There is little point in simply erecting a bird room, filling it indiscriminately with breeding cages of varying sizes and introducing the stock. The prime consideration must, of course, be the comfort of the stock, but it should also be considered that convenience and ease of working for the fancier have a bearing on the planning of a bird room.

Flights in which a number of birds are kept, while not strictly essential, are undoubtedly very desirable, and every effort should be made to incorporate these in the overall plan. If, as has been suggested, a small bird room is being built, then there are methods which can be used to overcome some of the problems. The importance of a flight, indoor or outdoor, is in its height, rather than its overall size. The larger the flight, of course, the better, but it should be stressed again that height is the important governing factor. The reason is that out of the breeding season, plenty of exercise is important to the birds, which is the reason for their being kept in flights, in which they have more room to fly around, which, in turn, helps to solve problems caused by their becoming overweight.

If the flights are built to their fullest possible height, then the birds will use more energy in flying up and down for their food and drink than they do in level flight. The least important aspect in building a flight is its width. If there is length and height, then that is sufficient. In a small bird room, such as that described, it is possible to manage with only one indoor flight. If this is built at one end of the room, perhaps 2 feet (61 cm) wide, and to the width and height of the room, such a flight will help to provide the hens with exercise. What then, of the cocks?

By using one's ingenuity the breeding cages, which will be described in detail later, can be made in units or blocks of as many single units as will fit into the available space. If the floors and the dividing partitions between the single cages are made in such a manner that they can be easily removed, such a unit can quickly be converted into a small flight at the end of the breeding season.

Position of the Cages

In breeding Budgerigars for exhibition purposes and the establishment of a true breeding line, it is essential that the birds should be paired with the mate chosen by the fancier, rather than birds being allowed to choose their own mates. If the birds are placed in their cages immediately prior to the breeding season, and the cocks and hens are able to see each other at relatively close quarters, it may well be that this situation could occur in any event. To overcome this problem, it is essential that the sexes should be separated by the full length of the bird room while in the flights, and that cages are not placed opposite each other across the narrow width of the room at the beginning of breeding operations. In a large bird room, this problem will probably not arise, but in a smaller structure, it may well cause problems for the fancier.

Unquestionably the best position for the breeding cages, and that favoured by almost all fanciers, is to place these along the full length of the long wall of the bird room, opposite the windows. This allows more light into the cages, which is important, especially in the breeding season.

OUTSIDE FLIGHTS

Most Budgerigar breeders have outside flights, which have a distinct advantage, in that the birds are not only able to obtain essential exercise, but also have the full benefits of abundant amounts of fresh air. The arrangement of such flights is not in itself important, but from an aesthetic point of view, it must be assumed that the fancier wishes his bird room to have as attractive an appearance as possible.

The usual method of building outside flights, which, again, should be as large as possible, is to build either one on each end of the bird room, or to have two flights along the front of the room, separated by the door. This method has further advantages, especially in a large bird room.

If the outside flights are built in that manner, and as outlined in *Figure 2.1*, the inside and outside flights can be interconnected by the simple expedient of opening the windows. This then has the effect of extending the size of the flight and also of allowing more fresh air into the bird room for birds which may be being kept in stock cages indoors.

All of the points mentioned should be kept firmly in mind when planning the bird room. For example, because of the proximity of the boundary fence, it may be possible to build larger outdoor flights if they are placed along the front of the bird room as described. It would be pointless to erect the bird room in its chosen position with the intention of building outside flights at each end, only to find that when the structure has been erected, there is some reason to prevent this. Such circumstances could possibly lead to the entire bird room having to be redesigned. It is clear then, that the planning stage is most important and the beginner in particular is very strongly advised to consider very carefully the design of his bird room before starting to build. Every decision taken at this stage will have some bearing on other aspects of building the bird room, and it is far better to discover any possible problems at this stage than during construction, or after the bird room has been erected.

General Layout

There are certain points which should be covered in terms of the general layout of the bird room, and these are perhaps best illustrated by *Figures 2.1* and *2.2*, which show suggested and very popular types of bird room favoured by many fanciers. *Figure 2.1* shows the layout for a larger type of room, and *Figure 2.2* a smaller version. The actual layout will, of course, be dependent upon the physical circumstances of the individual fancier, but my view is that the general layout shown in *Figure 2.1* is very close to the ideal Budgerigar breeding room.

Now having reached the point at which building can begin, it is important that the builder should be aware of the reasons for some of the built in features of the room being so precise.

Positioning of the Windows

The size and siting of the windows in the bird room are very important factors. The admittance of daylight is essential but, by the same token, it is possible to provide excess natural light. Equally, small windows are not desirable, and the result must be a compromise.

If, for example, the height at the front of the room is 7 feet (2.13 m) then a depth of window area of about 3 feet 6 inches (1.07 m) would be roughly correct. With larger windows, temperature control would be difficult, even if the windows are double glazed, and a smaller area might be inadequate.

An aid to ventilation which is becoming very popular among Budgerigar breeders, and breeders of cage birds in general, is the venetian blind type of glass ventilator which is fitted above the windows. These can be adjusted if for any reason the birds cannot be allowed into the outside flights either to exclude the cold in winter, or to provide better circulation of air in the summer.

It is not advisable to install windows at the ends of the bird room, because this will result in a lack of privacy for the sitting hens, and may cause rearing problems.

Positioning the Door

The positioning of the door of the bird room is very important. As we have seen, the windows should be installed along the full length of the front of the bird room and, if that is the case, this precludes that particular wall from being used for any other purpose, since to install breeding cages along the inside of the windows would completely defeat the object of the exercise by cutting down the amount of light.

That being so, we are then left with one long wall at the back of the room and two short walls, one of which, especially in the case of the smaller bird room will be needed for an indoor flight; this leaves only the one short wall clear and available for use. If the door is installed in the remaining short wall, this again, especially in the case of the smaller bird room, will effectively prevent its use for any other purpose.

The culmination of these points, is that the door should be installed in the centre of the front of the building, and should be constructed to open outward, again saving space in the interior. If this advice is followed, and the outside flights are built along the front of the bird room as suggested, there are other advantages which will be discussed later.

ERECTING THE BIRD ROOM

The design of the bird room having been completed, there is one point to which extremely careful attention must be paid, namely, the erection of the building. During the course of erection, every joint and corner must be inspected and double checked before further work is allowed to proceed. One of the major causes of disease in a Budgerigar breeding room is a draughty environment. Dampness is also a major cause of illness among the stock, and any source of either should be treated with the utmost caution. It is an undoubted fact that faults occurring during building will take far more time to rectify after the bird room is built than if they are treated during the course of construction, and great stress must be made of this point. As we shall see later, the fitting of an inner lining in the bird room is essential, and if faults are allowed to go unnoticed during the construction of the outer shell of the building, then a great amount of work and effort will be necessary if they are present after completion.

Another point to be considered is that the building should be lifted away from the ground, whether or not a concrete base has been laid. The best method of carrying out this particular exercise is to place the floor on top of old railway sleepers, which are usually available without difficulty.

Apart from the obvious advantage of preventing penetrating damp in the bird room, this method will also help to prevent the entry of rats or mice. It is also important at this stage to remember to treat the under-side of the floor very liberally with some type of rot preventative. Such an operation will be extremely difficult after the bird room has been erected and the point should be carefully noted.

Roof Covering

Most bird rooms have coverings of roofing felt, but the builder should be made aware that there are different grades of such materials. Only the thickest and best grade should be used. True, it will be more expensive, but its cost far outweighs the disadvantages of using the thinner material. Such material is difficult to work with, and is very easily torn. A slight break in the inner material may rapidly result in its being turn further in a high wind, and the total destruction of the whole of the roof covering.

When the roof is being covered, and after the edges have been nailed down with the correct type of broad headed felt nails, thin laths should be placed along the joints in the material, and nailed down very firmly. This will prevent the entry of water underneath the felt and consequently into the bird room.

While on the subject of fixing the roof, it should be pointed out that the practice of the installation of roof lights appears to be becoming increasingly popular among fanciers. These do have advantages in the sense of admitting more light, but they are not particularly easy to install, and my own view is that if the ordinary windows are of adequate size, then the additional time and trouble involved, not to mention the expense, is probably not justified.

Ventilators

It is at the stage at which the outside shell of the building is being erected, and before the inner lining is fitted, that the builder must consider the installation of adequate ventilation. Sometimes, especially during the winter months, it is inadvisable to have the windows open, but adequate ventilation is absolutely essential.

During the erection of the shell, a hole should be cut in one end of the building, low down near the floor. Another should be cut high up in the opposite wall, near the roof, and an adequate size for a 10 foot (3 m) by 8 foot (2.44 m) bird room would be roughly 10 inches (25 cm) square. On the outside of the bird room, laths should be placed across the length of the hole in a venetian blind kind of arrangement to stop the entry of rainwater and to prevent the wind blowing directly into the interior.

It is also advisable at this stage to decide at which point the electricity supply will enter the bird room, and to cut a suitably sized hole in the shell for that purpose.

Another task is to cut into the shell an opening or openings for the entrance to the outside flights for the birds. This will, of course, depend upon the siting of the flights. If it can be arranged, the holes should be placed in such a position that they can be opened or closed from outside the flight. One very easy method of providing this facility is to make the cover for the holes a sliding arrangement. It is then a simple matter to fix a metal bar on the cover which protrudes through the wire netting of the flight. It is, of course, essential to make sure that when the birds are locked up for the night, no draughts are caused by ill fitting covers over the so called bob holes.

Some difficulty may be experienced if the cocks are to be kept in converted cage units as suggested earlier, but there is a relatively easy answer to the problem. If the cage unit is placed at the other side of the bird room to the flight, a tunnel can be built from timber, to lead from an open cage door to the bob hole in the wall of the room. Surprising as it may seem, the birds will very quickly become accustomed to this method of getting into and out of the outside flight.

Lining the Bird Room

Having now reached the stage at which the outside shell has been erected, we are ready to proceed with the next step, which is to line the interior. Such lining is necessary, because if, as will be suggested later, electric heating is to be installed, the cost of heating an unlined bird room will be infinitely greater than in a lined room. Temperature will also be far easier to control if a lining is used.

The most widely used material for lining a bird room is hardboard, which is relatively inexpensive and easy to use. Plasterboard, while it may be suitable for other species, is certainly not suitable for Budgerigars, which have very strong and very destructive beaks. The birds would quite certainly demolish a plasterboard lining very quickly indeed, and the use of this material is most definitely not recommended. Similarly polystyrene can be very easily destroyed by the birds, and there is the added danger that it can, if used improperly, be a fire hazard. Having seen a house which had polystyrene lined ceilings after a fire, I am personally able to vouch for the accuracy of the latter statement.

A point which the builder might consider when lining the bird room with hardboard, is that the lining should be fitted by means of beading, as opposed to its being simply tacked to the bearers. Many fanciers use this method as a kind of insurance against the day when rodents might gain entry to the bird room. If the hardboard is fixed with beading, then it will be far easier to remove if the pests make their nests in the cavity between the inner lining and the outer shell of the building, which they inevitably will.

The cavity created by the installation of the inner lining should be filled with the fibreglass type of insulating material more normally used for the insulation of the lofts of houses. This will give added insulation and will also help to cut down on heating costs; it also helps to maintain an even temperature.

INSTALLATION OF HEATING

It is a fact that the installation of heating in a Budgerigar breeding room is not essential. Whether it is desirable is, however, a quite different matter. It would be true to say that Budgerigars can be, and for that matter often are, bred in unheated bird rooms. If, however, the breeder of exhibition Budgerigars intends to breed young stock for showing in the breeders' classes, especially at the early shows, then heating is an essential part of bird room management.

Owing to the now generally accepted practice of having young in the nest boxes by very early in January, some form of heating is essential. There is no necessity, however, to install a heating system capable of raising the interior temperature to very high levels. So long as the heating system is capable of raising and maintaining the interior temperature to 50 degrees Fahrenheit, there is no need for anything more elaborate.

The breeder must take care, however, in the type of heating which he decides to use. Under no circumstances should the paraffin type be used. Temperature control is completely impossible by the use of such methods, and there is an obvious danger in leaving a naked flame unattended. Another disadvantage, and a lethal disadvantage at that, is that if the level of fuel is allowed to drop, or the wick is untrimmed, such heaters have a pronounced tendency to smoke and to give off fumes which will very quickly fill the bird room and kill the stock. I must stress again, and most strongly, that under no circumstances must this type of heating be considered.

I have seen oil filled radiators used quite effectively in bird rooms, but

Figure 2.3   An Electric Heater which is most suitable for Budgerigar Bird Rooms

although this type of heater will certainly serve the purpose, they are quite expensive.

By far the most widely used and effective method of heating a Budgerigar breeding room, is by the use of tubular heaters. These are relatively inexpensive to buy, they can be obtained in almost any length required, and are probably the most suitable means available for the purpose.

The heaters come in two different ratings, of 60 watt and 80 watt. There is a formula by which means the precise amount of heating necessary to raise the temperature of any given space by one degree Fahrenheit can be calculated. For our purposes, however, it is sufficient to use the following: calculate the cubic capacity of the bird room by multiplying the length x breadth x height. For each 35 cubic feet of space, allow one foot of 60 watt heater, or 45 cubic feet for the one foot of 80 watt rated type. Provided this formula is followed, and the bird room is well insulated as described, the method should prove quite effective.

It should also be pointed out that the installation of the electricity supply from the house to the bird room is not difficult, but if there is any doubt, then professional advice should be sought.

If heating is being installed, there is one item of equipment which then becomes essential, namely, a thermostat.

The term **temperature control** has been mentioned several times up to this point, and it is this aspect of heating a breeding room which makes the installation of a thermostat an essential part of the electrical heating system. Without such a device, there is no control of the temperature at all, and no way of keeping the internal temperature down to acceptable levels.

A thermostat also has the added advantage, of course, of keeping costs down by switching off the electricity supply when the room temperature reaches the desired level.

Installation of Lighting

Similar remarks to those made on the heating system also apply to the installation of light. Certainly breeding operations can be carried out without the aid of artificial light, but if early breeding is the aim, then it is essential.

Artificial light, as we shall see later, is used to bring the birds into breeding condition, and is also used to give them sufficient time in any given 24 hours of light by which their chicks can be fed. There are several different types of lamp on the market, and the fancier will have to decide which type he wishes to install.

There are several types of fluorescent light, but the one most widely used and most strongly recommended by fanciers is the natural daylight

20

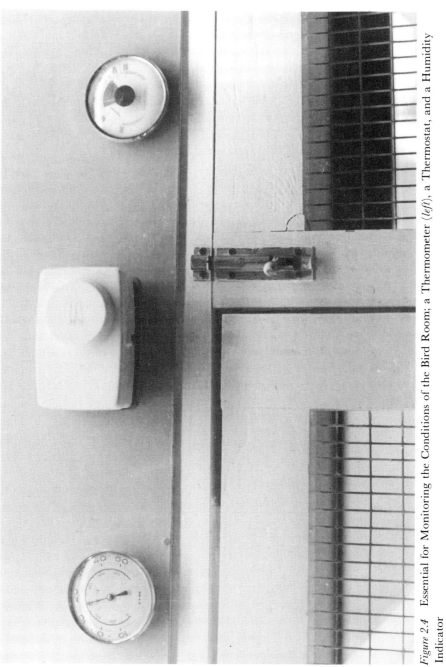

Figure 2.4   Essential for Monitoring the Conditions of the Bird Room; a Thermometer (*left*), a Thermostat, and a Humidity Indicator

type. It is generally considered that this type of lamp resembles natural daylight far more closely than any other type, and since one of the aims of keeping all types of birds is to adhere as closely as possible to the natural breeding patterns of the birds themselves, it would appear that this is the correct type of lamp to use.

When the lights are being installed, the best position is above the windows and away from the breeding cages. This will allow more light to enter the cages at floor level and will not make the birds afraid because of its proximity.

A useful, but perhaps expensive addition to the lighting system is a dimmer switch. While not essential, these appliances are most useful. Unfortunately, a dimmer unit will not work in conjunction with the daylight strip lamp type of lighting, and if such an appliance is being installed, then the more common tungsten type of bulb will have to be used. The difficulty can be overcome, however, by the use of two time switches. These can be set so that the daylight strip lamp is turned off, and at the same time, the ordinary tungsten light is turned on.

At that point, the dimmer unit, which is coupled to the tungsten system will dim down the lights in a reasonable facsimile of conditions which apply when dusk is falling. The birds will then fill up the crops of their brood for the night and go to roost in the normal manner.

There is, however, a cheaper method of carrying out the same procedure. Instead of simulating conditions of dusk in the evening, it is a simple matter to install a single time switch, set to operate at whatever time the fancier chooses before daybreak. By this means, the light will simply be turned on automatically, and turned off after full daylight has broken. The birds will then go to roost naturally at dusk.

It may be, of course, that the latter method of providing artificial light may not be acceptable to individual fanciers. If, for example, they are unable to feed their stock before leaving for work in the morning, then it will be dark by the time they return, and switching the light off suddenly can result in the birds going to roost with their crops only half filled. This aspect of Budgerigar management will be discussed later.

ERECTION OF THE FLIGHTS

We now have a bird room which is draught and damp proof, and which is adequately heated and lit; we must now consider the last addition to the actual structure of the bird room, the indoor and outdoor flights.

If the bird room is sufficiently large to accommodate two inside flights along the inside of the windows, as outlined in *Figure 2.1*, the easiest method of installation is to erect a 'shelf' of solid wood, plywood is

Figure 2.5   A closer view of an Outside Flight

probably best, from the corner of the room to the edge of the door. It is then a relatively easy matter to make three frames, one for each end and one running the length of the flight and covered with 1 inch (25 mm) x ½ inch (13 mm) galvanised wire netting. It will make the fancier's job much easier if the full length frame is divided into sections, each section being hinged to its neighbour. This will make the task of catching up any individual bird easier when this becomes necessary.

Erecting a flight at the end of the bird room as seen in *Figure 2.5*, is a very simple matter, and consists merely of making a frame to the size of the breadth and height of the room incorporating a door and covering this with wire netting.

The flights illustrated in *Figure 2.1* have an added advantage, in that the space beneath is then easily converted to cupboard space for the storage of equipment, show cages and so on.

Building the Outside Flights

An outside flight is nothing more than a large cage, and is easily constructed from four frames, fitted together and incorporating a door. Most fanciers, however, make a fifth frame, to cover the bottom of the flight, and this is set into the ground to a depth of about 1 foot (30 cm), and covered with ½ inch (13 mm) galvanised wire netting. This is a precaution against the entry of rodents, and is quite an effective deterrent.

There are two distinct theories on covering the floor of outside flights. One school argues that the birds may often be seen pecking at the soil, the inference being that they derive some benefit from so doing. Other fanciers, however, cover the bottom of their flights with small pebbles, which they say keeps the soil from becoming soured by the constant bombardment of the droppings of the birds, and that if this practice is followed, it is a simple matter to clean the floor of the flight by raking it over when necessary.

It would be foolish to guess at which is the more popular method, but it is certainly true that the birds do peck at the earth in flights in which they have the opportunity of so doing. Assuming that the birds know what they are about, my own view is that the floor of the outdoor flights are better left in their natural state. If the fancier then believes that the earth is becoming soured, it is a relatively simple matter to dig it over with a garden fork and turn up fresh earth.

One point which must be noted, is that the doors of outside flights must have a safety door; that is, a type of small porch with two doors. The porch is constructed in such a way that the fancier can enter it, closing the outer door behind him. He is then able to open the other door directly into the flight. The reasons for this are quite apparent and surely no explanation is necessary.

The breeder will also have to decide whether he should cover the tops of his outside flights. Many breeders do carry out this practice on the premise that the wild birds, which will be attracted to the aviary, can carry diseases which may then be transferred to the stock due to the outside flights becoming contaminated with the droppings of the wildlings. Some breeders compromise by half covering the roof of the flight, but in my view, this is completely defeating the object, since the uncovered area will be contaminated in any event. If the fancier is attempting to prevent the intrusion of diseases carried by wild birds, therefore, the only logical answer is to cover the roof of the flight completely.

PAINTING THE BIRD ROOM

There is little to be said regarding painting the outside flights. Creosote is undoubtedly the best treatment for the woodwork, but it should also be pointed out that attention should be given to the wire netting. This should be examined very carefully for signs of rust. It is by no means unknown for birds to be killed after picking up rust from deteriorating wire netting. If any rust is found, it should be cleaned with a wire brush. A check should be made for drips of galvanising, which could have the same effect if the birds are able to break them off and ingest them. After a careful check has been made, the wire should then be treated with black bitumastic paint.

So far as the exterior of the bird room is concerned, the only real question is whether to paint or creosote. The question is one of aesthetics rather than practicality, because either method will protect the woodwork quite adequately. If paint is being used, however, several good thick coats should be applied and the job should not be skimped under any circumstances. The advantage of painting, is that a painted bird room requires repainting perhaps every three years, whereas a bird room treated with creosote will require treatment at least every two years and possibly yearly.

My personal opinion is that a bird room which has been creosoted in a light shade presents a very smart and pleasant appearance, and the treatment of the woodwork with this substance will certainly help to dissuade the local rodent population from trying to gain entry. It is a fact that rodents have an aversion to the taste of creosote and will make little if any attempt to gnaw through wood which has been so treated.

It should also be pointed out at this juncture, that painting operations

25

should be carried out before the birds are installed. Paint fumes can be dangerous to the stock, and although in a well ventilated bird room any adverse effect is unlikely, it is perhaps better not to take the chance.

For the interior of the bird room, a good quality gloss paint is recommended. This type of paint is more durable than water based emulsions and will wear better and last longer.

Figure 2.6 A Breeding Cage *Courtesy:* **Cage and Aviary Birds**

26

CHAPTER 3

FITTING OUT THE BIRD ROOM

CAGES

For the purpose of breeding exhibition Budgerigars, individual stock cages are an essential part of bird room equipment. The use of such cages immediately before the breeding season begins will ensure that the birds will not become attached to the wrong partner, and will also allow the fancier to assess his stock on an individual basis. It is very difficult to try to assess the stock when they are flying around in a flight.

Many breeders who are setting up new bird rooms have their cages built in, with the back wall of the room forming the backs of the cages. This method does perhaps save a little time and trouble, and possibly expense, but it does have one very distinct advantage.

In, for example, a bird room perhaps 14 feet (4.27 m) in length and 7 feet (2.13 m) in height, a unit sufficiently large to fill all of the available space would be extremely large and cumbersome. It would most certainly be very heavy. To fill such a space, therefore, at least two, and probably three units would be required. As we have seen, it is advantageous to build the cages in such a manner that when the slides between the individual cages are removed, the full length of the unit becomes in effect, a mini flight, an especially useful item for use in caring for young stock.

The advantage of using units is that these can be moved around in the bird room if necessary, but I see no real advantage in building extremely large units, which would have to stand in the same position in the bird room at any event, purely because of their size.

My view, and I am sure that shared by most breeders, is that it is better to build the cages into the bird room. Another advantage of this method of installing cages is, of course, that all of the available space is taken up, and perhaps more importantly, used. If cages are being built in, then the reason for sound planning becomes obvious. When the cages have been installed in this manner, there is no way of moving them about, and, therefore, the importance of sound planning in the first instance assumes very great importance.

Cages are not difficult to make for the average handyman, but if they are being built in, with the aim of the slides and/or floors being removable for conversion to flights, some thought will have to be given to the actual construction.

The Basic Breeding Cage

A single breeding cage for exhibition Budgerigars should be not less than 2 feet (61 cm) in length, 15 inches (38 cm) in height and 15 inches in depth. These measurements apply especially if the nest boxes are to be placed inside the cages, of which more will be said later. Two feet is quite sufficient so far as the length of the cages is concerned, but if the 15 inch depth and height can be increased to 18 inches (46 cm), then so much the better.

The cage is in effect a box with an open front, covered with wire, and with a door 7 inches (18 cm) square at the minimum. At the bottom of the wire front is a rail, and beneath that is a drawer which is removable for easy cleaning. This is the basic unit on which cage units should be based and, if built in units are being made, then it is purely a question of how many such cages will fit into the available space. The builder of the built in unit has a distinct advantage here, in that sizes may be altered by perhaps an inch or two in order to accommodate more cages. It should also be pointed out here that the cages should not be down to floor level, but should be raised away from the floor by at least 10 inches (25 cm).

One point to which very careful attention must be paid when cages are being built is that all cracks, no matter how minute, should be filled with putty, plastic wood or some similar material before the cages are painted. If this is not attended to at the outset, and the breeder is unfortunate enough to be invaded with red or grey mite, parasites which infest bird breeding establishments given the opportunity and which we will discuss later, it is in these minute cracks where they will live during the day time, and from which they will be extremely difficult to dislodge.

Painting the cages with a good gloss polyurethane paint is essential. The birds will very soon strip off the lighter emulsion type of paint, and it is also essential to see that the lead based type of paint is *not* used. This type of paint could poison the birds, but since the polyurethane type mentioned above is readily available there is no reason why the lead based type should be used.

The colour of the cages may be important, depending upon the siting of the bird room. Most breeders paint the interiors of their rooms white, but it should be pointed out that in hot weather, and with relatively large windows, the temperature may become excessively high. This being so, and assuming that the bird room has been placed facing south, as suggested, the fancier may wish to consider painting his bird room and his cages in some light pastel shade. The point is not very important, but note should be made of it.

Perches

The cages and flights will need perches, and there are several types. Taking the cages first, each should have two perches, $\frac{1}{2}$ inch (13 mm) in diameter set from front to back of the cage. One of the perches should be set at an angle of about 45 degrees to give the birds exercise for the feet and legs.

Some fanciers provide one square perch and another round or oval, for the same purpose. Square perches are also used in the breeding season, of which more will be said later.

Perches in the flights are usually made in a ladder formation, with the width almost the full width of the flight. They are very easy to make, consisting of two side pieces through which holes are drilled, and dowelling is passed through and secured. When installing such perches, however, make sure that the angle is not too steep, resulting in the birds on the lower perches having their plumage soiled by the droppings from the birds above.

Feeding Pots

There are several different types of feeding pots, but most fanciers offer seed in open dishes. The automatic type of feeder is useful, in that these do not require to be filled every day, but they do have disadvantages.

The type of feeder in the form of a plastic tube which clips to the outside of the bars of the cage front is quite effective as a water container. When this type of utensil is used for seed, however, the trough can quickly become blocked with seed husk, preventing the seed from flowing down. The fancier will no doubt have noticed that Budgerigars, like most other birds, feed frequently, but with only small amounts being taken at one time. This underlines the fact that Budgerigars require regular feeding, and if they are not able to obtain food, they will die relatively quickly. Thus, the use of such seed dispensers as described above is not recommended.

Seed hoppers are also frequently used in Budgerigar breeding establishments, but when these are bought, or made, then a careful

Figure 3.1   Plastic drinker (*top*) and galvanised bird bath, Manufactured by Geo. H. Elt Ltd.

30

check should be made to make sure that the seed flows well and that the outlet cannot become blocked with husk.

Similar remarks apply to the type of seed feeder which utilises an upturned jam jar. These can be very effective and labour saving, but again, some types are better than others, and care must be taken.

Whether the staple diet is offered in the type of feeder described above or not, open dishes will be required in order to feed soaked seed and other tit-bits to the birds. A dish of about 4 inches (10 cm) in diameter and $1\frac{1}{2}$ (3.8 cm) to 2 inches (5 cm) deep would be adequate for the purpose.

Water Pots

The plastic tube type of drinker already described is the one most widely used by fanciers and is excellent for the purpose. The up-turned jam jar is also excellent, but since they hold relatively large amounts of water, they are more suited to use in the flights than in individual cages.

Giving water in open dishes is not recommended, because the water will quickly become contaminated by sawdust or sand from the cage floors, or by seed husk and so on.

Grit Pots

Smaller open dishes will be required for the purpose of offering grit. This, as we shall see, is a very important part of the diet of Budgerigars and must be available at all times.

CLEANING EQUIPMENT

During cleaning, the fancier will no doubt become aware very quickly of the difficulties of removing dried excreta and so on from the cage floors. The use of a metal wallpaper scraper will undoubtedly remove stubborn substances, but their use is not recommended. The result of using tools of that nature will be that the cages will require painting at least three times each season, and using a plastic scraper, while it may not be quite so efficient, will certainly prevent damage to the paintwork of the cages.

Vacuum Cleaner

If one has the cash available, the use of an industrial heavy duty vacuum cleaner is a great help during the cleaning out process. With such an appliance, it is a very simple matter to run the birds into their show cages, take off the wire front, and clean out the cage very quickly. Whether one wishes to go to the expense is, of course, a matter for the individual to decide, but I have seen this method of cleaning in use, and I

Figure 3.2 A Humidifier which is particularly useful when the eggs are due to hatch

Figure 3.3   A very useful aid to ventilation is this type of Window

33

can positively vouch for the fact that it saves a great deal of time, especially if one has relatively large numbers of cages to clean.

EXTRACTOR FAN

Many fanciers have extractor fans fitted in their bird rooms. I have mixed feelings on this subject. If, as has been suggested, the windows are made to open, and an adequate ventilation system is installed, then I really do not see the need.

One distinct advantage of such an appliance, however, is that it is undoubtedly an aid when cleaning out is taking place. Budgerigars generate very large amounts of dust, and when cleaning is going on, the atmosphere in the bird room can become somewhat overpowering, especially in very cold weather when it is not possible to leave the doors or windows open. In such circumstances, an extractor fan is extremely helpful.

WIRE DOOR

If, for some reason, the outside flights must be built on the ends of the bird room, a wire door which fits inside the solid door is a desirable aid to ventilation, especially during summer. This consists simply of a frame to fit the doorway, covered with wire netting. Its use is surely obvious.

PROTECTED GLASS

The fancier should also note that he may wish to protect any windows or glass panelled doors which are not already covered by the flights being built in front of them. This applies especially when the bird room is sited close to the edge of the garden where there may be children playing. It is a simple matter to tack a little wire netting over unprotected windows, and may save quite a lot of trouble if an accident should occur.

TRAINING CAGES

A unit of training cages will be required. Show cages are becoming very expensive, and their use for training purposes in the bird room, during which process they will be damaged, certainly by having the paint chipped if nothing worse, is not to be desired.

A much better method of training young birds is to build a unit of cages with the same dimensions as those of a **Budgerigar Society** Show Cage, the specifications for which appear on pages 125-7. Show cage perches should be used, and although the cages may not be precisely the same, in that they will probably be square as opposed to their having a

Figure 3.4   A Training Unit such as this one is a very useful piece of Bird Room equipment

sloping roof, this type of cage will certainly help the young birds to become accustomed to show cage conditions.

A unit of perhaps twelve or sixteen such cages can be fitted to the end wall of the bird room and will most certainly be a very useful addition to the general equipment. The interiors of these cages should, of course, be painted white as are the show cages.

STORAGE BINS

The question of seed storage is important. It is a fact that damp seed will sour extremely quickly, contaminating a whole batch with alarming rapidity. Because of this, seed should never be stored for any length of time in the bags in which it is delivered. The size of the container will depend upon the number of birds kept and the amount of seed being stored, but if large amounts are kept, then the smaller type of plastic dustbin complete with lid is very suitable. For smaller amounts, plastic buckets or similar containers may be used, but the important point is to make sure that these are covered. Such containers are a very important part of bird room equipment.

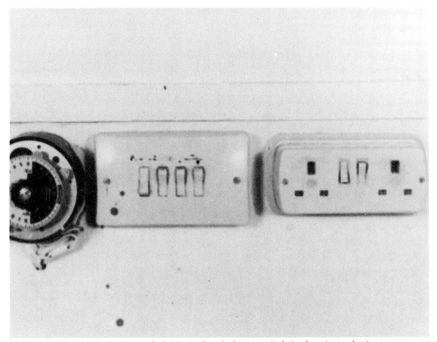

Figure 3.5 A neat layout of plugs and switches, and, *left*, the time clock

CHAPTER 4

FEEDING

DIET

Before any stock is obtained, it is absolutely essential that the beginner should know something of the diet of the Budgerigar. It is often said that a Budgerigar will survive if it is fed on seed and water and nothing else, and this is very probably accurate. What kind of condition such a bird would be in, and how long it could thrive under such conditions are, however, quite different questions.

It is true that seed is the basis of the diet of a Budgerigar, but the bird needs quite a number of different types of food if it is to be kept healthy and happy, and in good condition for breeding and exhibition purposes.

The most important word, so far as the efficient feeding of a stud of Budgerigars is concerned, is without doubt **balance**. Any diet, for Budgerigars, or any other form of life, must contain a balance between the wide variety of constituents, especially the chemical constituents of substances such as manganese, potassium, vitamins and so on. If an imbalance is created, then trouble will follow without question, and probably very quickly. It follows, therefore, that the fancier should be aware of the constitution of the various foods and seeds which may be offered and must then work out for himself a basic diet which is adequate for the purpose, and which his birds will accept readily. It should perhaps be noted here that this last point may bear closer examination. Simply because a bird is said to prefer a particular food or seed because of its species, is certainly not to say that this is the case. Many canary fanciers believe that canaries will not eat millet spray, but I know of two canary breeders who feed such seed to their birds regularly, and I can confirm with certainty that the birds will attack a new spray immediately it is placed in their flight. So much for theory!

Figure 4.1 Feeding Pots containing *left* Mixed Seed, *centre* Mineralised Grit, *right* Plain Canary, and *top* Whole Oats

The fancier may be far better employed in finding out for himself what type of diet his birds prefer, and so long as that diet is known to have a good balance of the basic elements, and the birds are thriving upon it, I see no reason to change simply because it is not accepted to be 'the done thing'. Caution is advised, however, and I would certainly not advise the reader to experiment with different foods while excluding food of known value and which he knows that the birds are eating well.

BASIC GENERAL INGREDIENTS

Before beginning to break down the various seeds and foods into their constituent parts, the reader should understand that there are three basic parts to the diet of all living things. All foods have these basic constituents in differing quantities, and again, a reasonable balance must be maintained between them. The three elements are proteins, carbohydrates and fats. It should be made clear that the protein and fats referred to as being part of the dietary needs of Budgerigars are vegetable, as opposed to animal proteins and fats, which are quite different.

Protein

Protein is a most essential part of the diet of Budgerigars, especially for breeding hens and growing chicks. This is the substance which develops muscle and size in the birds, giving stamina and strength and, in the case of breeding hens, helping them to maintain their body weight while going through the process of feeding their young. In the case of young chicks, protein is required to help them grow and build up their body weight. Protein is also very essential to adult birds when in the moult, and to young chicks for a different reason.

The feathers of all birds are composed almost entirely of proteins, and at such times as those mentioned above, when the birds are growing feathers, much of their protein intake is being used up by the body for that purpose. Meanwhile, the normal bodily functions are taking place, weight is probably being lost because of exercise and needs to be replaced, certainly so far as the adult birds are concerned, and the consequence of all of this is that at such times, a protein enriched diet should be given.

Proteins in themselves cannot be used by the body. They are extremely complicated structures, and their basic ingredients, for want of a better expression, are amino acids, of which there are several hundred. Each amino acid is used for some very specific purpose within the body structure, but until certain other substances are mixed with the proteins within the body itself, the basic protein cannot be broken down.

Figure 4.2 Automatic Seed Hopper (*top*) and Drinking Cup, Manufactured by Geo. H. Elt Ltd.

To illustrate the point, let us take the analogy of cement. Sand, cement mixture and water all have the potential of becoming cement. Not until the three ingredients are added together, however, will that substance be formed. Also, the finished cement will be unusable if the three constituents are not added in the correct quantities.

The connection between cement and the feeding of Budgerigars may seem a little tenuous, but the rules are precisely and exactly the same. None of the constituents of either diet, or cement, is of any use without the others, and what is more, in the correct quantities. Because of its complicated make up, this is especially true of protein.

Fortunately for Budgerigar breeders, however, the amounts of amino acids required are so very minute in relation to the amount of protein required in the diet, that for all practical purposes, it may fairly be said that given a well balanced diet, the essential amino acids will be present in sufficient quantities.

Many fanciers appear to believe that Budgerigars are absolutely vegetarian, but such is not the case — when meat bones are given to birds the strands of meat are quickly picked clean. There is also evidence to suggest that Budgerigars in the wild take animal protein in the form of insects. Another method of feeding animal protein especially during the breeding season which is becoming very popular among fanciers, is the feeding of turkey starter crumbs. The methods of feeding extra animal protein to the birds will be discussed when we come to the chapter on breeding.

Carbohydrates

The carbohydrate content of the diet is that part which provides energy. In effect, the substance 'burns up' excess fats and proteins, and a fair demonstration of this would be to point out that if the birds are fed on a normal protein diet, but without sufficient carbohydrates, excess protein, which, remember, is used for muscle building would not be used, especially if the birds are not obtaining exercise. The result of that situation would be that the birds would put on weight and become obese, spoiling them for both the show bench and for breeding purposes.

In the breeding season, however, extra carbohydrate is helpful, especially to the parent birds, since they are using up more energy than is normal in the extra effort of feeding their young. A very good method of providing extra carbohydrates is in the use of sprouted seed. When a seed begins to germinate, it undergoes changes which in effect turn the starch content of the seed into fructose, a very digestible form of carbohydrate, which is almost instant energy.

41

Fats

Fats are a supplement to the carbohydrates in effect, and provide energy and especially body heat. Oily seeds, as for example niger and linseed are important sources for vegetable fats, which is the reason for the inclusion of these types of seed in tonic and condition mixtures.

Like the carbohydrates, however, plants produce comparatively little fat, and other methods must be found for supplying these substances at certain times of the year, especially in the breeding season. This is a relatively easy matter in relation to additional protein or carbohydrate, and again this will be discussed later.

BASIC DIET

That part of the diet of Budgerigars which is usually referred to by fanciers as **the basic diet**, is generally taken to mean the seed mixture which the birds are offered daily. Other additions, soaked seed, soaked groats and so on, are usually referred to as **additives**.

As we have seen, the all important factor in the diet as a whole is balance, and this being so, it follows that before we can start to work out a balanced overall diet, including additives, the basic diet must be as well balanced as possible.

In order to do this, we must first know what is contained in any given seed, and in what proportions. It seems, however, that seed analyses rarely, if ever, agree exactly. Despite that fact, the table below gives what I consider to be the probable constitution of the seeds listed, and certainly it is sufficiently accurate for our purposes:

ANALYSIS OF SEED VALUES

	Protein	Carbo-hydrate	Fat	Water
Canary Seed	14.0	52.0	5.50	15.0
Millet Seed	15.0	57.0	4.0	14.0
Rape Seed	22.0	20.0	40.0	7.0
Linseed	23.0	23.0	24.0	9.0
Niger Seed	21.0	22.0	40.0	12.0
Maw Seed	19.0	18.0	45.0	9.0
Hemp Seed	16.0	25.0	30.0	11.0
Lettuce Seed	1.0	2.0	0.2	95.0
Wheat	11.0	2.0	70.0	15.0

Seed Mixture

The basic seed diet usually fed to Budgerigars consists of four parts canary seed, one part each of white and yellow millet and one half part of groats, which are oats from which the husks have been removed. Many fanciers, however, give different seeds separately, with the exception of tonic or condition mixtures, and put canary seed in one dish, millet in another and so on. The latter method probably results in less wasted seed, but may also result in the birds feeding from only one type of seed, which, as we have seen, is a very undesirable state of affairs.

This basic diet is relatively well balanced, but, certainly, it needs to be supplemented by additives. There is nothing to suppose, for example, that the birds will readily take all the seeds included, particularly if they are offered separately and, therefore, some method must be found of ensuring that they obtain the necessary supplements, whether they like it or not. Fortunately for the breeder, there are some very simple methods of ensuring that every bird takes in essential dietary elements. Before we consider these methods, however, we must first consider what substances are required.

ADDITIVES

Grit

The constant supply of grit to Budgerigars is absolutely essential, and the grit pots must be kept full at all times. Neglect of this aspect of feeding will certainly result in the birds being underfed, and consequently underweight and listless.

The reasons for the importance of grit to the diet are really quite simply explained. In humans and animals, food must be broken down into a semi-liquid mass before it can be assimilated into the body through the stomach and intestines. Those creatures having teeth have no problems in this respect, it is purely a matter of placing the food in the mouth and grinding it by means of the teeth which nature has provided for that express purpose. Birds, however, to state the obvious, do not have teeth, and must, therefore, use some other means of changing the food into a softer state, and one in which it can be more easily assimilated. In order to do this, the birds take in grit. This, together with the food or seed is passed into the crop, a sac like organ which is found at the front of the base of the throat.

In the crop, the mixture of seed and grit is churned around until the seed is broken down and may be passed into the stomach to be further broken down. If grit is not provided, the fancier is actively preventing the bird from chewing its food, and in a secondary sense, is not providing sufficient nourishment because the bird is unable to derive the full benefit from its diet.

Grit also performs another very valuable function, in that it is a very good source of vital minerals, calcium, magnesium and so on. This is especially valuable during the breeding season when the hens need relatively large amounts of calcium to form the shells of their eggs.

Some fanciers prefer to use only oystershell grit, while others prefer to use a mixed grit which has been developed especially for the purpose by seed firms. In my view, the latter is the best course of action, because in a mixed grit there are probably far more trace elements and minerals than in a grit which contains only one substance, rich in minerals though that may be.

VITAMIN ADDITIVES

The addition of vitamins to the diet is also very important, and there can be very few serious breeders of exhibition Budgerigars who do not give vitamin supplements to their birds.

Specific vitamins have very specific purposes, and it is useful for the breeder to know what these purposes are and what the effect on the birds will be by either over or underfeeding each one.

Vitamin A

Vitamin A is found in milk, butter, eggs, especially carrots and, so far as Budgerigar breeders are concerned, in large quantities in cod liver oil. It is also found in a number of green vegetables, especially in spinach. It is used by the body in the assimilation of food and general metabolism and has a distinct bearing on the functions of glands, as for example the lymph glands and similar glands. It also has an effect on the conditions of the skin and is a well known factor in preventing diseases of the nervous system as, for example neurasthenia.

Vitamin B1

Otherwise referred to as Thiamine, this vitamin is an important substance found in milk, eggs, and especially yeast and cereals. Its main function is to react to carbohydrates, allowing that substance to be correctly used by the body processes. The vitamin can be given to Budgerigars in proprietary yeast mixtures produced by manufacturers of specialist Budgerigar foods as, for example, in P.Y.M.

Vitamin B2

This substance helps to break down protein products in the same way as B1 breaks down carbohydrates. Without it, protein cannot be correctly broken down. Again, perhaps fortunately for breeders of exhibition Budgerigars, it is found mainly in the seeds of plants of all types but especially in cereals and grasses.

Vitamin B12

Very great care must be taken if it is decided to provide this specific vitamin to the diet, as the amount needed by cage birds is minute, and the over provision of it can do great harm. My advice is to leave the provision of this substance to nature, which, if a well balanced diet is given will provide quite sufficient quantities. It is true to say that some fanciers do give this vitamin in a proprietary form obtainable from chemists, but I believe they are misguided and I would very strongly advise against such practices. It should perhaps be pointed out at this juncture, that the over provision of vitamins can cause equally as much trouble, if not perhaps more, than their under provision, and so minute are the required quantities that care must be taken when providing all of those listed here.

Other vitamins in the B Complex, include **Niacin**, **Folic Acid** and **Riboflavin** among others. Each has a specific purpose, but again, yeast is a good source of these vitamins, and if P.Y.M. or some similar dietary additive is given according to the maker's recommendations, this will certainly be quite sufficient.

Vitamin C

This essential vitamin is found especially in citrus fruits, and in black-currant in particular. It is also found in greenfoods and its lack produces scurvy. This fact was discovered in the days of sailing ships, and British sailors were given limes to eat, with which to make up the deficiency. This has nothing to do with the breeding of Budgerigars of course, but the reader may find the fact of interest, since it was from this period that the British became known as 'Limeys'.

Vitamin D

This is another of the balancing substances needed in order that other substances can be correctly assimilated. In the case of Vitamin D, this applies to the use of calcium and phosphorus by the body processes, and this is especially important in young chicks. It is from Calcium, which we will discuss later, that bones are formed, and the lack of sufficient quantities of Vitamin D will cause rickets in adults and young alike, but more especially in the young because their bones will not form correctly, but will be bowed. Like Vitamin A, Vitamin D is found in large quantities in cod liver oil, but in common with other additives, the over provision of Vitamin D can, and frequently does cause serious illness in the stock, especially in the gastro intestinal tract.

Vitamin E

Vitamin E is found in seeds, in the same manner as Vitamin B2. Known as the fertility vitamin, Vitamin E certainly has a bearing on the

45

prevention of sterility in Budgerigars, and for this reason, many fanciers give a mixture of cod liver oil with added wheat germ oil, which is a particularly good source of this substance.

MINERALS

Minerals are equally important to the diet as vitamins. Again, the emphasis must be on balance, and under or over provision will cause problems which can be directly attributed to that cause. Although mineral salts are essential to the diet, almost all are present in sufficient quantities in the normal diet as outlined later, and making special provision for adding these substances to the diet is, in my view, not only superfluous, but downright dangerous. For example, an over provision of iodine may well result in a condition known as thyrotoxicosis, which occurs in humans when the thyroid gland at the base of the neck begins to produce more iodine than is required.

The main minerals which are required are: **sodium**, **iodine**, **potassium**, **magnesium**, **phosphorus**, **sulphur**, **iron** and **copper**. Most of these minerals are to be found in greenfoods, which is logical, since greenfoods take their nourishment from the soil, which is of course rich in such substances which are absorbed by the growing plants. Some plants are richer in certain of these substances than others. For example, water cress and chickweed have a particularly rich iron content. Cereals are especially rich in phosphorus, and almost all plants contain traces of the other minerals mentioned, certainly in sufficient quantities for our purposes.

The one very important mineral which we have not mentioned, is **calcium**. This mineral has been singled out because of its great importance to growing chicks and to hens which need extra calcium just before and during the breeding season.

It is from calcium that the bones are formed and the lack of sufficient calcium for breeding hens will result in the production of soft shelled eggs, which, in turn, will cause egg binding and the possible death of the hen. The birds will take in a certain amount of calcium from their normal supply of grit; cocks and hens alike should also have extra calcium available.

Extra calcium is usually offered in the form of cuttlefish bone, a substance which is very close to being pure calcium. The bone may be hung up in the flights or stock cages, and special clips are available from pet shops for this purpose.

Another good source of calcium which the birds will enjoy, is in the form of crushed egg shells. These should be dried under a grill and crushed with a baking roller, following which they are then offered to the birds. Offering crushed egg shell serves a dual purpose, in that the shells are rich in mineral salts other than calcium, and are a valuable source of these substances.

OILS

We have already noted that cod liver oil is rich in Vitamins A and D among others, and that wheat germ is rich in Vitamin E. All three are important to the diet, and there is a very easy method of supplying them to the stock.

To each pound (454 g) of seed, add one teaspoon of cod liver oil with added wheat germ oil. Mix this very thoroughly, and although the quantity may seem small, the entire contents of the mixing bucket will be very quickly coated. After mixing, the contents should be left for 24 hours before it is given to the stock, thus ensuring that the seed has had time to absorb the oil.

When the seed is being mixed in this manner, however, take care not to mix too much at one time, especially in the summer months. Cod liver oil will turn rancid very quickly, especially in hot weather, and if given to the stock in this state, it will cause gastric and intestinal troubles.

For those vitamins which are not to be found in cod liver oil, there are two methods of provision. One is to use a proprietary yeast mixture, which as we have seen contains a number of vitamins, another to provide extra vitamins by the addition of soluble liquids to the water supply.

The latter method is very easy to carry out and is widely adopted by many breeders. My own view, however, is that the method is of doubtful value. The substance popularly used is 'Abidec', a proprietary vitamin solution which is added to the water at about three drops to each water fountain. The question must arise, however, that when such a tiny amount of liquid is added to a comparatively large amount of water, and when only a small proportion of the water is actually consumed by the birds, whether the addition of such substances is effective, and will the birds be receiving sufficient quantities?

Clearly, many breeders believe that the birds are receiving sufficient vitamin additives by this means, but I must repeat that I am somewhat sceptical of the value of this method.

In my opinion, a much better method is to offer dietary mineral and vitamin supplements in the form of the yeast based powders already mentioned. P.Y.M. is one which I have used and which I have always found to be perfectly suitable. The use of this method also ensures that the birds are taking in most of the proferred supplement, ingesting it from the husk of the seed with which it is mixed.

If the fancier decides to offer the liquid supplements, care must be taken, and the amounts set down here should not be given more than three times each week. The results of overfeeding with these substances have already been described.

WATER

The provision of clean, fresh water daily is absolutely essential. As with seed, close observation will show that Budgerigars drink frequently but only a little at a time. Depriving them of water will certainly cause them distress, and although it may be true to say that they would not necessarily die, they would certainly be distinctly unhappy.

Some fanciers take the extra precaution of boiling all the water given to the stock. I believe, however, that they are certainly in a minority, and I also believe that this practice is carrying things a little too far. I have certainly never carried this out, and so far as I am aware, neither have I ever lost a bird because of it.

It may be of value to add a very tiny pinch of salt to the water pots in order to supply certain minerals, but if the fancier is to supply whole-meal bread as will be suggested later, then I do not believe that to be necessary.

GREENFOOD

Budgerigars love greenfood, there can be no doubt of that, but as in all things associated with the breeding and rearing of these birds, a little moderation is necessary.

The best plants to be given are the wild varieties, and especially dandelion and chickweed, both of which the birds will eat avidly. Care must be taken when collecting such plants, because there is a danger that they may have been contaminated with insecticides or other forms of chemical spray.

It should also be pointed out that wild plants should not be collected from hedgerows or verges close to fields which have been sprayed, because the substances used in spraying can be carried relatively long distances by the wind. If there is any doubt in this respect then the plants should be left and another source found.

Domestic vegetables may be given: cress, lettuce, cabbage and sprout leaves, and a favourite among Budgerigar breeders, spinach. With the brassica types of vegetables, however, care must be taken, as over provision may cause scouring of the bowel.

No matter what type of vegetable is being given, wild or otherwise, it should always be given fresh. Wild plants must be thoroughly washed before being offered, and no greenfood should be left in the cages or flights for more than a day.

If fresh greenfood is not available, a good substitute is grated carrot, although not all birds will eat this. The birds also enjoy apple, and although this may have little food value, there is no doubt that it is relished by most birds and can be offered as a tit-bit in order to put a little variation in the diet.

SOFT FOOD

This type of food will be required during the breeding season for the purpose of rearing the chicks. Breeders will no doubt note that when the parents are feeding the chicks, they take the food into their own beaks, pass this into the crop, changing its consistency to a yellowish milky type of substance. It is then regurgitated and passed to the chicks. It follows that it is much harder for the parents to carry out this exercise, if all they have to work on is hard seed. Soft food is much more easily converted and makes the job of feeding the chicks that much easier for the hen. There is also the point that soft food, because of its constitution, is very high in protein which, as we have seen, is essential to growing chicks, and feeding soft food is an excellent method of ensuring that the chicks are receiving sufficient quantities.

Many breeders give soft food only during the breeding season or, at best, only just before the start of that period. My view, however, is that it is better to give soft food once each week throughout the year. We have already discussed the reasons for giving soft food and, clearly, if the parent birds do not take in soft food, this will not be passed on to the chicks.

I believe that if the adult birds are given the food once each week, they will become accustomed to it, and will probably look upon it as a tit-bit. If that assumption is correct, and I see no reason to believe otherwise, then it is far more probable that they will accept such food with alacrity when the feeding of it becomes necessary.

Preparation of Soft Food

The basis of soft food in earlier times was usually breadcrumbs, but fanciers have stopped this practice since it was discovered that artificial colouring agents and so on are used in white bread, and this can cause health problems in the stock. Using wheat germ breadcrumbs is quite acceptable, but there are on the market at present foods developed by the specialist bird food firms which are perfectly sound, and I would advise the use of one of these for the purpose.

Fanciers use all kinds of concoctions of their own devising in their soft food mixtures. Honey and glucose D are favourites which are used, presumably to provide extra energy. I have nothing against such additions, but whether the addition of such substances is necessary, and whether by adding them an imbalance is being created is in my view a very debatable point. It would be true to say, however, that very many fanciers adopt these methods very successfully. The question of whether they should be added is one which the fancier will have to decide for himself on the evidence presented.

Assuming that a proprietary brand of soft food is being used, one hard boiled egg should be mixed to every two tablespoons of food. With these quantities, water is not necessary because the food will absorb the water content from the egg. The egg should be shelled, and the white and yolk are then grated or passed through a kitchen sieve. After that, the mixture should be very well blended together, and the honey or glucose added if desired.

Some fanciers also add powdered skimmed milk to their soft food mixture, a powder which is high in protein content, and again, I see nothing wrong with the practice.

If glucose, skimmed milk or honey are added, then to the quantities mentioned, that is one egg to two tablespoons of food, only one teaspoonful of any other additive should be given. Although there is nothing wrong in adding such substances, we must return again to the all important balance.

While on the subject of soft foods in general, there is an important point which should be noted. In the summer months especially, when the temperature of the bird room will be relatively high, soft foods containing hard boiled egg or milk will sour far more quickly than in normal or colder temperatures. Because of this, soft food should not be left in the cages for long periods, and it should also be noted that in higher temperatures egg or milk can sour in a matter of hours, and such foods which have been placed in the cages perhaps early in the morning may well become sour by early afternoon. Such food should be changed regularly, and if there is any doubt in the mind of the breeder that it may be soured, then it should be discarded immediately and fresh food prepared.

Wholemeal Bread and Milk

Many fanciers give their birds wholemeal bread once each week, because this type of food contains certain salts which are not found in other foods. A one inch cube of bread soaked in milk is sufficient for one pair of birds, and certainly most birds enjoy this variation to their normal diet.

If it is decided that this method is to be adopted during the breeding season, then it is better to give the birds bread and milk once each week for the same reasons as those given for the provision of soft food.

SOAKED SEED

Soaked seed and soaked groats are also given, especially during the breeding season. We have already discussed the reasons for soaking seed, but during the breeding season such seed is also much easier to convert to crop milk than hard seed.

If soaked seed is to be given, and I suggest that it should, then one must consider whether giving additional glucose to the birds as a part of their soft food diet is really necessary. We have seen that there is additional glucose present in germinated seed, and in my view, this should be sufficient during the breeding season, in relation to the overall diet and should give sufficient extra glucose without the dangers of creating an imbalance in the diet as a whole.

Seed can be germinated very easily by using the following method. Place the seed in a suitable container (large shallow dishes are best), and cover with water. Allow plenty of water because the seed tends to soak up large amounts. Leave the seed for 48 hours to soak, then remove it, straining well and washing thoroughly through a fine mesh sieve. After washing, allow the excess water to drain off, put the seed into a shallow dish and place in a warm, dry place for 48 hours. The airing cupboard is ideal. After 48 hours, take the seed out and thoroughly wash again, and it will be found that the seed will have begun to germinate and to split open; it may then be offered to the birds.

When soaking seed, it is better not to soak too much at any one time. The best method is to put in only sufficient seed for one day's supply. On the day after the first batch of seed has been put in to soak, begin the next batch and so on. This method will result in the fancier having seed which is ready to be fed to the birds after four days, seed which is germinating, and seed which is soaking, thus creating a continuous progression with soaked seed always available. This is especially important in the breeding season.

Tonic Seed

Once or twice each week, a proprietary tonic seed can be given. These mixtures, which contain seeds not found in the normal diet, linseed, teazle, rape and so on, are developed by the seed companies especially for the purpose and are an excellent tonic and conditioner aimed at keeping the birds in the best of fitness and general health. They provide some of the minute 'doses' of minerals and trace elements not in the

51

normal diet and thus are an important part of the overall feeding programme.

THE WEEKLY DIET

Having discussed all of the different varieties of foods normally offered Budgerigars, we must now discuss how these are to be offered to provide a balanced diet throughout the week. It should be made quite clear that this does not apply to the diet during the breeding season, which is another matter entirely.

The basic diet of four parts canary seed, and half a part each of white and yellow millet to which cod liver oil with wheat germ oil has been added is given daily.

Grit: the grit pots should be examined daily, and refilled when necessary.

Water: the water pots should be refilled daily, whether there is sufficient water to last the day or not.

Greenfood: should be given every alternate day in small quantities.

Vitamin Supplements: Abidec or some similar preparation may be added to the water fountains at the rate of three drops in each fountain twice weekly, or a yeast mixture may be added to the basic seed diet at the rate of one teaspoon of powder to one pint of seed, but not both.

Soft Food: should be given once weekly.

Tonic Seed: may be given in small quantities twice each week.

Such a diet would ensure that the birds are obtaining all their nutritional requirements and would keep them in good health. It should be pointed out that the additions to the diet should be given on different days.

Before leaving the subject of feeding, there are one or two other points which need discussion.

BIRDS AS INDIVIDUALS

Not the least of these points is that the birds are individuals in all things. Just as some birds will enjoy flying out in hot bright sunshine, while others prefer the shade, so some bird will enjoy one type of food, while ignoring other foods which other birds enjoy immensely.

In this respect, the fancier must find out by observation what one bird prefers in relation to another. If, by some chance, the particular bird does not enjoy a type of food which the breeder believes would be advantageous, then some other means of supplying that form of food must be found.

In general, it will be found that most birds will eat all of the foods referred to here, but I have known birds, for example, to refuse completely to eat bread and milk, though it should be stressed these have been extremely rare occurrences. In such cases, however, alternative methods of supplying essential dietary requirements must be found.

SEED QUALITY

This is an extremely important point, and great attention must be paid to it. It is a fact that reputable seed companies with standards which must be kept up would not supply seed which is of inferior quality. It is frequently found, however, that seed is on offer locally at much reduced prices. It may well be that such seed is good, sweet seed with fat kernels, but the buyer should be very wary indeed.

Recently, I have had two examples of fanciers being given cause to regret buying cheap seed. In one case, a friend had troubles because of his birds dying off for no apparent reason. They lost weight rapidly and were usually found dead in the stock cages in the early morning. My friend tried all kinds of methods to overcome the problem, and after this had happened several times, he finally sent the body of one of his birds to an avian post mortem service. He was astounded when he received the report which, in effect, said that the bird had died from starvation and vitamin deficiency. He then sent a sample of the seed he had been using to a laboratory for tests, and was not quite so surprised when the report returned, announcing that the seed had very little, if any, food value at all.

In another case, a friend bought cheap seed, along with a number of members of a local society. He used the seed for about a week, and then, on visiting the bird room of another friend whom he knew was using the same seed, he was somewhat surprised to find the same seed, but in a different bag. On reaching home, he went into his own bird room and examined a bag of seed, upon which was printed in small rubber stamped letters 'recleaned'. No wonder the seed was cheap.

DRIED MEAT

One practice which appears to be becoming more widespread recently, is that of feeding grated dried meat to Budgerigars. The meat is ground or grated into a powder and is mixed with the soft food or seed before being offered to the birds. This is undoubtedly a good method of providing extra animal protein to the birds, but I am not at all sure that it is advisable. Recent research has shown that feeding meat to exhibition Budgerigars has the effect of making them carnivorous and cannibalistic. The practice may well also lead to hens becoming destroyers of eggs or chicks, assuming the previous statement to be true.

It is undoubtedly a fact that giving raw meat to dogs as opposed to cooked meat makes them much more aggressive, and as I firmly believe that giving meat to Budgerigars has much the same effect, this method of feeding is not recommended until much more is known about the effect.

GRASS SOD

Another practice adopted by many fanciers is to supply the birds with a small cube of grass sod once each week. The birds will certainly peck the grass and the soil, the theory being that, as wild birds peck at the soil, obviously deriving some benefit from it, so cage birds will derive similar benefit. Provided the grass is clean and not soiled by animal droppings, I see nothing wrong with this idea. If this method is to be used, then a small cube of about one inch is sufficient for each bird.

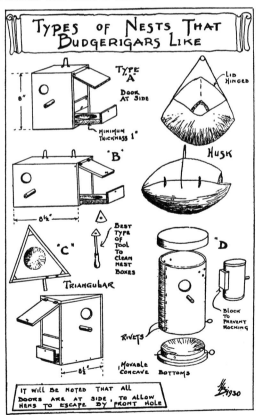

Figure 4.3 Types of Nest Boxes as seen in an old book

CHAPTER 5

DAY TO DAY MANAGEMENT

Before we go on to discuss the birds themselves, it is essential that the beginner should know something of the day to day management of a Budgerigar bird room, and of the importance of some of the points raised.

CLEANLINESS

In my view, there is no subject more important in the day to day management of a bird room than cleanliness. If the bird room is dirty, then disease will have ideal conditions in which to breed, which it unquestionably will, and the result will be weak, unhealthy stock which will be quite unsuitable for either breeding or showing.

Food and water pots especially should be kept scrupulously clean, and it is important to establish a daily routine for that purpose. Make sure that there is plenty of time set aside each day for the cleaning of the bird room, sweeping up and so on, and that if it is necessary there is also time to clean feeders and drinkers. At any event, both food and water pots should be thoroughly washed and cleaned at least twice each week at the very minimum.

When the water pots are being cleaned and refilled, pay special attention to the areas immediately around or beneath them. The birds will spread the odd few drops of water around, and if these are left to soak into the woodwork, they will eventually become permanently damp and will create a damp and humid environment where the organisms which cause disease will find ideal breeding conditions. There is also the point, of course, that if the cage bottoms are allowed to remain permanently damp, the wood will develop wet rot and will need replacing far more quickly than otherwise.

Cleaning the Bird Room

During cleaning operations, every item of equipment being used should be washed with a disinfectant solution and allowed to dry thoroughly before being replaced in the cage or flight. This applies to such items as perches, seed dishes and so on.

The important word in this respect is thoroughness, and there is little point in, for example, cleaning out a cage, washing it if necessary and leaving the perches in a dirty condition.

FRESH AIR

Most fanciers, I believe, would agree that when the birds are not in the process of breeding, they should be allowed into the outside flights at every conceivable opportunity. This applies in winter and summer, and many fanciers use the method of keeping the windows of the bird room closed during the winter, but open the bob-holes to allow the birds outside if they so wish. Provided that there is no frost about and the day is reasonably fresh, then there is nothing at all wrong with this practice. Common sense must be used a little here, however, and the birds should not be allowed out when it is too cold.

Another point upon which I believe most fanciers would agree, is that the birds should not be allowed outside if there is fog about. This can lead to chest troubles and allowing the birds outside in those conditions is not recommended.

STORAGE OF LIQUIDS

Liquids of any description should never be stored in a bird room unless it is absolutely unavoidable. I have quite literally lost count of the numbers of stories I have been told about birds being drowned in paint, water, and in one case, in an open topped bucket of creosote. If by any chance a bird should escape from its cage or flight and there is an open topped container in the bird room, it is almost certain that the bird will eventually find its way in. If the storage of liquids is unavoidable for any reason, then these should be covered at all times and should be kept fastened away in a cupboard.

NOISES

Some breeders of exhibition Budgerigars apparently believe that they should tip-toe around the bird room without a sound. I do not believe that for one moment, nor, I suspect, does any experienced breeder. Remember that when a bird is taken to a show, especially for the first time, it will be subjected to sights and sounds which it has never experienced before. Certainly it will be seeing a large crowd of people in very close proximity. Because of that, the fancier should behave in the bird room in his own natural manner, making no more or less noise than he would normally. One should, of course try to avoid loud and unusual noises which may startle the birds, especially during the breeding season, but it is certainly not advisable to creep silently around the bird room.

Noises at night are an entirely different subject, however, and any possible source of such noises should be tracked down and eliminated. While it is true that the birds will soon become familiar with, for example the noise of passing trains if one happens to live close by a railway line, they may well become very frightened by unfamiliar noises.

Such noises are not always apparent to the breeder, for example, a loose piece of wire tapping on the flight outside or a tree branch tapping on the outside of the bird room may be interpreted by the birds as being the entry of a cat or a rat. If the birds are disturbed by noises at night, they may fly blindly around in their cages or flights and may damage themselves in the process.

A good idea is for the fancier, perhaps twice a week, to spend a few minutes just before dark, sitting quietly in the bird room to detect such noises.

CATS

Cats can, and frequently are, a great nuisance to bird breeders. As already stated, they will sit for hours on nearby fences or similar vantage points watching the birds in the flights or the bird room. A favourite perch is on top of the flight or the bird room itself.

There is, however, a very well proven and widely adopted method of dealing with this nuisance. If the cats are sitting on top of a fence or the bird room, knock in a row of nails along the fence or around the perimeter of the roof. Leave the nails protruding by about two inches (5 cm), and then twist thin wire or string around the nail heads, along the fence, or to form a criss cross pattern over the roof. This is a very effective method of dealing with the problem.

SPRAYING FOR MITE

A part of the regular routine of any bird room, should be preventative measures against red or grey mite, which were referred to earlier. A once monthly spraying with a preparatory anti-mite spray of both birds and the bird room will prevent these pests from gaining a foothold and attention should be given to this point as a regular part of the general management programme.

Many fanciers hang up fly killers for the same purpose, and it appears that a popular favourite is **Vapona**. Whether this does effectively kill off parasites in the bird room which may be some distance away from the fly killer, I do not know, nor am I prepared to comment one way or the other. My opinion is that even if such a method is used, I would certainly continue regular spraying with the appropriate substances.

Vermin

Rats and mice can become a problem if they are allowed to gain entry into the bird room. If the bird room is creosoted, then the problem will probably not arise in any event, unless the actual fabric of the building is allowed to fall into disrepair. If vermin do gain entry, however, then every possible course of action which can be taken should be adopted, as a matter of urgency.

If mice are present, then, as already stated, they will almost certainly make their nests in the space between the inner and outer walls. They will be almost impossible to dislodge once they have become established, and if that is the case, troublesome though it may be, the inner lining of the bird room must be removed and all of the pests killed.

If it is believed that they have gained entry very recently, then traps can be set, but make sure that these are of the type which catch them alive. A spring loaded mousetrap is not able to differentiate between an escaped Budgerigar and a mouse!

The exclusion of vermin cannot be stressed sufficiently strongly. They will certainly frighten the birds at night, rats will kill the birds if they are able to catch them, and seed and food will be contaminated with equal certainty, causing disease among the stock and probably the death of valuable birds.

CAGE FLOOR COVERING

Most fanciers use sawdust or cleaned sand for covering the floors of the stock or breeding cages, but recently, a disturbing fact has come to light regarding the use of sawdust. Apparently, timber merchants are now in the habit of using preservative treatments which are poisonous to birds. I have heard several stories recently of fanciers losing birds under circumstances which appear to indicate this as the probable cause. I have no personal experience of this problem, but since the sawdust which I use comes from a local timber merchant, as opposed to a subsidiary of one of the larger companies I may have been fortunate. Certainly the problem bears thinking about, and it may be better at the

Figure 5.1   Budgerigars cannot always be persuaded to Bathe, and an effective alternative is to Spray them in the Flights

present time for the fancier to use good quality washed sand rather than sawdust for floor coverings until the matter is resolved one way or the other. Loose floor covering of the types mentioned are needed because without them, the droppings of the birds will adhere to the surface of the bottom of the cage and will be extremely difficult to detach without rubbing off the painted surface.

CHECKING THE BIRD ROOM

Because of what has been said previously about rats and mice, the fancier is strongly advised to check the building at least once each week. It takes only a few moments to walk around the outside and to examine the bird room for signs of rodents trying to gain entry. If any signs of cracks developing between the planks are found, then these should be dealt with immediately, which will serve a double purpose. Firstly, it will make life difficult for the rodents and, secondly, it will prevent rain-water from entering the wall cavity, causing the bird room to become damp.

BATHING

Plastic baths which fit on to the outside of an opened cage door are available from pet shops, and these are a valuable addition to the bird room. Most birds love a bath, and Budgerigars are no exception. It is not true, however, that any bird will immediately leap into a bath of water when it is provided, and if that is the case, then other means will have to be adopted for keeping the birds clean.

The answer is quite simply to spray the birds with the spray used for show preparation, which will be discussed later. While it may be true that not all birds will jump into a bath, it is true to say that Budgerigars in particular love to be sprayed. If this is done in the flight, most birds will come to the point at which the fancier stands and will stick out their chests, almost literally asking to be sprayed.

Birds should never be sprayed in the stock cages, however, and if the birds being so kept require spraying, then they should be removed into an old show cage or to a specially constructed spraying cage which is made completely from wire especially for the purpose. If one can be obtained, an old Border Canary or Yorkshire Canary show cage will be ideal.

ESTABLISHING A ROUTINE

A routine for feeding and cleaning should be established, and, like the feeding programme, when this has been achieved it should be adhered to at all costs. The times at which the individual fancier feeds or cleans his birds will, of course, depend upon his own circumstances and will be governed by such matters as the time he must leave for work and so on.

The times at which the birds are fed or attended to are not important, provided that they are strictly kept. It is always a great temptation to 'put it off until tomorrow', but in terms of the efficient management of a stud of exhibition Budgerigars, such an outlook is fatal. If the normal routine is changed by putting something off until tomorrow, then it only becomes another step to put off the same matter for two days, and so on. The consequences of that situation are, I am sure, only too obvious. Neglecting stock in that manner can only lead to inferior results, and possibly even more serious consequences. If the fancier begins to find that he is struggling to maintain his stock on a day to day basis, then the time has come to ask himself the question, 'am I over stocked', or perhaps even, 'am I right to continue looking after livestock when I have not the time to do it correctly?'

APPLIED INTELLIGENCE

Liberal amounts of good old fashioned common sense are required in a Budgerigar breeding room. It should be quite obvious that birds should not be sprayed late at night and allowed to go to roost with wet plumage, or that food which is known to have low keeping properties, like egg or milk, should be taken out of the stock cages or flights before they are allowed to become stale and possibly cause disease. Equally, it should be obvious that a badly fitting window or door should be repaired immediately so that draughts are eliminated; the list is endless.

The individual fancier will come across problems which will be peculiar to him because of his circumstances, and there will be no set pattern or recommended method of overcoming these. In those circumstances, he will have to use his intelligence and answer the questions for himself.

So far as general management is concerned, however, I repeat the comments made concerning the feeding programme. When a routine has been established which suits primarily the birds, and secondly the fancier, then do not change it no matter what anyone says. If the fancier wishes to experiment, then so be it, and quite right too, but it would be a foolish man who suddenly changed a successful routine for an experimental system the outcome of which is doubtful.

CHAPTER 6

BUYING THE INITIAL STOCK

There are two distinct schools of thought concerning the purchase of the initial breeding stock. One theory has it that the beginner is wise to buy several pairs of mediocre birds with which he is able to gain experience of breeding, while the other argument states that it is better to begin with perhaps only four pairs of good quality birds, on the assumption that any birds bred from such stock will at least give the newcomer a chance of success on the show bench. Although both theories have their supporters, I believe that it is true that the latter argument is the view held by most fanciers, and certainly I would support it. If the beginner buys mediocre stock, then the possibility of breeding good birds from that stock is extremely small and the result will be a lack of success on the show bench, a loss of interest on the part of the fancier, and possibly the loss of another potentially good fancier to the fancy as a whole.

PRICE

If, then, the newcomer to the fancy decides to opt for the purchase of only a few pairs of birds, the question of price must be raised. This is a very difficult subject, because any bird, no matter whether the buyer is an absolute beginner or a long established expert, is only worth the money which the buyer is prepared to pay for it. In general, there are good birds to be bought at around £10 to £15 at present, but it seems at the moment that the prices being asked for absolutely top quality birds are of the order of £100 and upward. Very high quality birds bred by breeders with outstanding reputations on the show bench also change hands quite frequently for much higher figures, and on one occasion some years ago, the breeder of the **Best Bird in Show** at the National Exhibition of Cage Birds was said to have been offered £500 by a Japanese breeder for the bird.

ADVICE AND WHAT TO BUY

With prices such as those being bandied about, the newcomer cannot be blamed for being thrown into a state of some confusion. Fortunately, there is a very easy answer, and one which is given to beginners by almost all established breeders.

First, join the local Budgerigar or Cage Bird Society, and having done so, find out who the respected fanciers are, not, mark, those who have been successful, but those who are respected by their fellow fanciers. It is quite probable, of course, that the fancier who is successful is also well respected by his peers. There are almost always a few such people to be found in every club, and the usual expression used by other fanciers to describe them is: 'a true fancier'. This is generally accepted to infer that the person concerned is interested not only in his own success, but for the reputation and continued success of the fancy as a whole.

When such a person has been found, the beginner can do no better than to put himself entirely in the hands of such a mentor. Usually, such people are more than willing to help the beginner by supplying good quality birds at reasonable prices, and one often hears it said that quality birds are often 'given away'. The term is used metaphorically, of course, and the beginner should not enter into negotiations expecting to buy the best birds in the bird room for next to nothing.

Usually, when a breeder produces a very high quality bird, he will not sell under any circumstances, unless he is perhaps offered some outrageous figure for the bird, and I suspect that, even then, he may well have second thoughts.

Probably the best for which the beginner can hope, is to obtain good quality birds, capable of reproducing good quality young, at a reasonable price. If the beginner has placed himself in the hands of a reputable breeder of long standing, then the chances of his being supplied with poor quality stock at inflated prices are quite remote.

I would certainly not advise the beginner to buy his birds through the fancy Press. Such a course could lead to disaster, unless the advertiser is known to the fancier concerned or has a high reputation among other club members. In any event, buying birds without seeing them first is always a hit and miss affair and is certainly not advisable.

A PICTURE OF THE IDEAL

Before setting out to purchase stock, the beginner should have at least some idea of what the ideal Budgerigar looks like.

All Budgerigars are judged to the same set of *standards*, a **scale of**

In the ideal Budgerigar we have a bird standing at the correct angle of thirty degrees from the vertical, with neatly fitting and well tucked-in beak, and good forward rise and upward lift of skull sweeping over to an excellent back-line. The eye is well placed, alert and fearless, and there is a good deep mask with well rounded and evenly spaced spots set not too high on the mask. The markings fall back from the eye to give that greatly desired free-from-ticking look which is so important. Excellent width of face is clearly indicated as is thickness of neck. The breast-line is right, conveying just enough depth to give a proper balance overall. Nicely cut away between the legs, this bird stands just sufficiently high above the perch. The wings are cushioned neatly on the body giving an uninterrupted line from head to tip of tail.

Figure 6.1   The Budgerigar Society Ideal — Side View *Courtesy* The Budgerigar Society

THE BUDGERIGAR SOCIETY'S SCALE OF POINTS

REVISED SCALE OF POINTS **Remember: condition is essential**	Size shape balance and deportment	Size and shape of head	Colour	Mask and spots	Wing markings
Green (Light, Dark or Olive)	45	20	15	15	5
Grey Green (Light, Medium or Dark)	45	20	15	15	5
Yellow (incldg. Op. Yell. but excldg. Lutino)	45	20	35	—	—
Olive Yellow (including Cinnamon Olive Yellow)	45	20	35	—	—
Skyblue, Cobalt, Mauve or Violet	45	20	15	15	5
Grey (Light, Medium or Dark)	45	20	15	15	5
White (Light Suffusion including Opaline White but excluding Albino)	45	20	* 35	—	—
Whitewing (Skyblue, Cobalt, Mauve, Violet or Grey)	45	20	* 35		
Yellow-wing (Light, Dark, Olive or Grey Green)	45	20	* 35	—	—
Greywing (Light, Dark, Olive or Grey Green)	45	20	10	10	15
Greywing (Skyblue, Cobalt, Mauve, Violet or Grey)	45	20	10	10	15
Cinnamon (Light, Dark, Olive or Grey Green)	45	20	10	10	15
Cinnamon (Skyblue, Cobalt, Mauve, Violet or Grey)	45	20	10	10	15
Fallow (Light, Dark, Olive or Grey Green)	45	20	15	15	5
Fallow (Skyblue, Cobalt, Mauve, Violet or Grey)	45	20	15	15	5
Lutino	45	20	35	—	—
Albino	45	20	35	—	—
Opaline (Light, Dark, Olive or Grey Green)	40	20	† 25	10	5
Opaline (Skyblue, Cobalt, Mauve, Violet or Grey)	40	20	† 25	10	5
Opaline Cinnamon (Light, Dark, Olive or Grey Green)	40	20	† 25	10	5
Opaline Cinnamon (Skyblue, Cobalt, Mauve, Violet or Grey)	40	20	† 25	10	5
Opaline Greywing (Light, Dark, Olive or Grey Green)	40	20	† 25	10	5
Opaline Greywing (Skyblue, Cobalt, Mauve, Violet or Grey)	40	20	† 25	10	5
Yellow-faced (All varieties in Blue series except Pieds)	45	20	15	15	5
Pied (Dominant varieties)	45	20	§ 15	10	‡ 10
Pied (Clear Flighted varieties)	45	20	10	10	★ 15
Pied (Recessive varieties)	45	20	‡ 20	—	‡ 15
Dark-eyed Clear varieties	45	20	35	—	—
Lacewings	45	20	10	10	15
Crested or Tufted varieties	40	■ 35	10	10 ●	5 ●

*Points allocated for depth of colour and clearness of wings.
†Including clear mantle and neck (10 points).
‡Including contrast in variegation.
★Including clear flights and tail.
§Includes band.
■Including crest or tuft.
●Varieties not having wing markings and throat spots will have the points allocated to colour.

Teams of six birds of any one colour or teams of four birds of any one colour.
Points: general quality, 50; uniformity, 50.

points, which is drawn up by **The Budgerigar Society** and against which each bird is compared. The official *standards* are reproduced here by kind permission of **The Budgerigar Society**.

This, then, is the scale of points as laid down by **The Budgerigar Society** in relation to the colour and markings of the different types of bird. Obviously this gives no indication, no mental picture, of what the ideal Budgerigar should be. It is therefore necessary to have a set of *standards* by which judges can be guided and, as with the scale of points, against which *standards* all birds are judged:

Condition — Essential; if a bird is not in condition it should never be considered for any award.

Type — Gracefully tapered from nape of neck to tip of tail, with an approximately straight back line, and a rather deep, nicely curved chest.

Length — The ideal length is 8½in (216 mm) from the crown of the head to the tip of the tail. **Wings** well braced, carried just above the cushion of the tail and not crossed. The ideal length of the wing is 3¾in (95 mm) from the butt to the tip of the longest primary flight, which must contain seven visual primary flight feathers fully grown and not broken. No bird showing 'long flighted' characteristics shall be eligible to take any award.

Head — Large, round, wide and symmetrical when viewed from any angle; curvature of skull commencing at cere, to lift outward and upward, continuing over the top and to base of head in one graceful sweep.

Beak — To be well set into face.

Eye — To be bold and bright, and positioned well away from front, top and back skull.

Neck — To be short and wide when viewed from either side or front.

Wings — Approximately two fifths of the total length of the bird, well braced, carried just above the cushion of the tail and not crossed.

Tail — To be straight and tight with two long tail feathers.

Position — Steady on perch at an angle of 30 degrees from the vertical, looking fearless and natural.

Mask and Spots — Mask to be clear, deep and wide and where demanded by the *standard* should be ornamented by six evenly spaced large round throat spots, the outer two being partially covered at the base by cheek patches, the size of the spots to be in proportion to the rest of the make up of the bird as shown in the illustrated Ideal. Spots can be either too large or too small.

Legs and Feet — Legs should be straight and strong, and two front and two rear toes and claws firmly gripping perch.

Markings — Wavy markings on cheek, head, neck, back and wings to stand out clearly.

Colour — Clear and level and of an even shade.

COLOUR STANDARDS

Having now seen the Colour and Ideal *Standard*, the beginner must be given some idea of what colour he is looking for in a bird of that description. The Society also has a set of descriptive standards for colour in the same way as those for size, deportment and so on. These are as follows:

Light Green — Mask: buttercup yellow, ornamented by six evenly spaced large round black throat spots, the outer two being partially covered at the base by cheek patches. **Cheek patches:** violet. **General body colour:** back, rump, breast, flanks and underparts bright grass green of a solid and even shade throughout. **Markings:** on cheeks, back of head, neck and wings, black and well defined on a buttercup background. **Tail:** long feathers, bluish black.

Dark Green — As above but with dark laurel green body colour. **Tail:** long feathers, darker in proportion.

Olive Green — As above but with a deep olive green body colour. **Tail:** long feathers, darker in proportion.

Grey Green — The Grey Green conforms to the standard of the light green except in the following details. **Cheek Patches:** grey to slate. **General body colour:** dull mustard green. **Tail:** long feathers, black. (It should be noted that there are light, medium and dark shades of Grey Green.)

Light Yellow — Mask: buttercup yellow. **Cheek patches:** silvery white to very pale pinkish violet. **General body colour:** back, rump, breast, flanks and underparts, deep buttercup yellow and as free from green suffusion as possible. **Primaries and Tail:** lighter than body. **Eye:** black pupil with white iris.

Dark Yellow — Same as above but correspondingly deeper in colour.

Olive Yellow — As above, but with mustard body colour.

Grey Yellow — As above but with a dull mustard body colour. (It should be noted that there are light, medium and dark shades of Grey Yellow.)

Skyblue — Mask: clear white, ornamented by six evenly spaced large round black throat spots, the outer two being partially covered at the base by cheek patches. **Cheek patches:** violet. **General body colour:** back, rump, breast, flanks and underparts, pure skyblue. **Markings:** On cheeks, back of head, neck and wings, black and well defined on a white ground. **Tail:** long feathers, bluish black.

Cobalt — As above but with a deep rich cobalt blue body colour. **Tail:** long feathers, darker in proportion.

Mauve — As above but with a purplish mauve body colour with a tendency to a pinkish tone. **Tail:** long feathers, darker in proportion.

Violet — As above but with a deep intense violet body colour. **Tail:** long feathers, darker in proportion.

Grey — Mask: white, ornamented by six evenly spaced large round black throat spots, the outer two being partially covered at the base by cheek patches. **Cheek patches:** grey/blue or slate. **General body colour:** back, rump, breast, flanks and underparts solid grey. **Markings:** on cheeks, back of head, neck and wings, black and well defined on a white ground. **Tail:** long feathers, black. (It should be noted that there are light, medium and dark shades of grey.)

White — Mask: white. **General body colour:** back, rump, breast, flanks and underparts, white (suffused with the colour being masked). **Wings and tail:** white, bluish or light grey. (It should be noted that there are blue, cobalt, mauve, violet and grey shades in both light and dark suffusion.)

Opaline Light Green — Mask: buttercup yellow, extending over back of head and merging into general body colour at a point level with the butt of wings where undulations should cease thus leaving a clear **V** effect between top of wings so desirable in this variety, to be ornamented by six evenly spaced large round black throat spots, the outer two being partially covered at the base by cheek patches.

67

Cheek patches: violet. **General body colour:** mantle (including **V** area or saddle), back, rump, breast, flanks and underparts, bright grass green. **Wings:** to be the same colour as body. Markings should be normal with a suffused iridescent effect. **Tail:** long feathers, not to be lighter than mantle.

Opaline Dark Green — As above but with dark laurel green body colour. **Tail:** long feathers, not to be lighter than mantle.

Opaline Olive Green — As above but with an olive green body colour. **Tail:** long feathers, not to be lighter than mantle.

Opaline Grey Green — As above but with a dull mustard green body colour. **Tail:** long feathers, not to be lighter than mantle. **Cheek patches:** grey to slate. (It should be noted that there are light, medium and dark shades of opaline grey green.)

Opaline Skyblue — **Mask:** white, extending over back of head and merging into general body colour at a point level with the butt of the wings where undulations should cease thus leaving a clear **V** effect between the top of wings so desirable in this variety, to be ornamented by six evenly spaced large round black spots, the outer two being partially covered at the base by cheek patches. **Cheek patches:** violet. **General body colour:** mantle (including **V** area or saddle), back, rump, breast, flanks and underparts, pure skyblue. **Wings:** to be the same colour as body. **Markings:** should be normal with a suffused iridescent effect. **Tail:** long feathers, not to be lighter than mantle.

Opaline Cobalt — As above but with a cobalt body colour. **Tail:** long feathers, not to be lighter than mantle.

Opaline Mauve — As above but with a mauve body colour. **Tail:** long feathers, not to be lighter than mantle.

Opaline Violet — As above but with a deep intense violet body colour. **Tail:** long feathers, not to be lighter than mantle.

Opaline Grey — As above but with a solid grey body colour. **Cheek patches:** grey to slate. **Tail:** long feathers, not to be lighter than mantle. (It should be pointed out that there are light, medium and dark shades of Opaline Grey.)

Opaline White — As for White but with a suggestion of Opaline characteristics.

Opaline Yellow — As for Yellow but with a suggestion of Opaline characteristics.

Opaline Cinnamon Light Green — **Mask:** buttercup yellow, extending over back of head and merging into general body colour at a point level with butt of wings where undulations should cease, thus leaving a clear **V** effect between top of wings so desirable in this variety, to be ornamented by six evenly spaced large cinnamon brown throat spots; the outer two being partially covered at the base by cheek patches. **Cheek patches:** violet. **General body colour:** mantle (including **V** area or saddle), back, rump, breast, flanks and underparts, pale grass green. Wings to be same colour as body. **Markings:** should be normal cinnamon brown with a suffused opalescent effect. **Tail:** long feathers, not to be lighter than mantle.

Opaline Cinnamon Dark Green — As above, but with a light laurel green body colour. **Tail:** long feathers, not to be lighter than mantle.

Opaline Cinnamon Olive Green — As above but with a light olive green body colour. **Tail:** long feathers not to be lighter than mantle.

Opaline Cinnamon Grey Green — As above but with a pale grey green body colour. **Tail:** long feathers, not to be lighter than mantle. **Cheek patches:** grey to slate. (It should be noted that there are light, medium and dark shades of Opaline Cinnamon Grey Green.)

Cinnamon Skyblue — **Mask:** white, ornamented by six evenly spaced large round cinnamon brown throat spots, the outer two being partially covered at the base by cheek patches. **Cheek patches:** violet. **General body colour:** back, rump, breast. flanks and underparts skyblue, 50 per cent or more of normal body colour. **Markings:** cheeks, back of head, neck and wings cinnamon brown on white ground and distinct as in normal colour. **Tail:** long feathers, blue with brown quill.

Cinnamon Cobalt — As above but with pale cobalt body colour. **Tail:** long feathers, cobalt with cinnamon shade.

Cinnamon Mauve — As above but with pale mauve body colour. **Tail:** long feathers, mauve with cinnamon shade.

Cinnamon Violet — As above but with pale violet body colour. **Tail:** long feathers, violet with cinnamon shade.

Cinnamon Grey — As above but with pale grey body colour. **Cheek patches:** pale grey. **Tail:** long feathers, pale grey with cinnamon shade. (It should be noted that there are light, medium and dark shades of Cinnamon Grey.)

Greywing Light Green — **Mask:** yellow, ornamented by six evenly spaced large round grey throat spots, the outer two being partially covered at the base by cheek patches. **Cheek patches:** pale violet. **General body colour:** back, rump, breast, flanks and underparts grass green, 50 per cent or more of normal body colour. **Markings:** on cheek, back of head, neck and wings should be light grey and distinct as in normal colour. **Tail:** long feathers, grey with pale bluish tinge.

Greywing Dark Green — As above but with a light laurel green body colour. **Tail:** long feathers, darker in proportion.

Greywing Olive Green — As above but with a light olive green body colour. **Tail:** long feathers, darker in proportion.

Greywing Grey Green — As above but with a light mustard green body colour. **Cheek patches:** light grey. **Tail:** long feathers, dark grey. (It should be noted that there are light, medium and dark shades of Greywing Grey Green.)

Greywing Skyblue — **Mask:** white, ornamented by six evenly spaced large round grey throat spots, the outer two being partially covered at the base by cheek patches. **Cheek patches:** light violet. **General body colour:** back, rump, breast, flanks and underparts skyblue, 50 per cent or more of normal body colour. **Markings:** on cheek, back of head, neck and wings should be light grey and distinct as in normal colour. **Tail:** long feathers, greyish blue tinge.

Greywing Cobalt — As above but with a pale cobalt body colour. **Tail:** long feathers, darker in proportion.

Greywing Mauve — As above but with a pale mauve body colour. **Tail:** long feathers, darker in proportion.

Greywing Violet — As above but with a pale violet body colour. **Tail:** long feathers, darker in proportion.

Greywing Grey — As above but with a pale grey body colour. **Cheek patches:** pale grey. **Tail:** long feathers, dark grey. (It should be noted that there are light, medium and dark shades of Greywing Grey.)

Opaline Greywing Light Green — **Mask:** yellow, extending over back of head and merging into general body colour at a point level with butt of wing where undulations should cease, leaving a definite **V** effect between top of wings so desirable in this variety, to be ornamented by six evenly spaced large round grey throat spots, the outer two being partially covered at the base by cheek patches. **Cheek patches:** violet. **General body colour:** mantle (including **V** area or saddle), back, rump, breast, flanks and underparts, pale grass green. Wings same colour as body. **Markings:** should be normal and light grey in colour with suffused opalescent effect. **Tail:** long feathers, smoky grey.

Opaline Greywing Dark Green — As above but with a light laurel green body colour. **Tail:** long feathers, darker in proportion.

Opaline Greywing Olive Green — As above but with a light olive green body colour. **Tail:** long feathers, darker in proportion.

Opaline Greywing Grey Green — As above but with a light mustard body colour. **Cheek patches:** light grey. **Tail:** long feathers, dark grey. (It should be noted that there are light, medium and dark shades of Opaline Greywing Grey Green.)

Opaline Greywing Skyblue — **Mask:** white, extending over back of head and merging into general body colour at a point level with the butt of wings where undulations should cease, leaving a definite clear **V** effect between top of wings so desirable in this variety, to be ornamented by six evenly spaced large round grey throat spots, the outer two being partially covered at the base by cheek patches. **Cheek patches:** violet. **General body colour:** mantle (including **V** area or saddle), back, rump, breast, flanks and underparts, pale skyblue. Wings same colour as body. **Markings:** should be normal and grey in colour with suffused opalescent effect. **Tail:** long feathers, grey.

Opaline Greywing Cobalt — As above but with pale cobalt body colour. **Tail:** darker in proportion.

Opaline Greywing Mauve — As above but with pale mauve body colour. **Tail:** darker in proportion.

Opaline Greywing Violet — As above but with pale violet body colour. **Tail:** darker in proportion.

Opaline Greywing Grey — As above but with pale grey body colour. **Cheek patches:** light grey. **Tail:** long feathers, grey. (It should be noted that there are light, medium and dark shades of Opaline Greywing Grey.)

Yellow Wing Light Green — **Mask:** buttercup yellow. **Cheek patches:** violet. **General body colour:** back, rump, breast, flanks and underparts, bright grass green. **Wings:** buttercup yellow, as free from markings as possible. **Tail:** long feathers, bluish. (**Note:** clearwings showing opaline characteristics should be shown in the A.O.C. or V class.)

Yellow Wing Dark Green — As above but with a dark laurel green body colour. **Tail:** long feathers, darker in proportion.

Yellow Wing Olive Green — As above but with an olive green body colour. **Tail:** long feathers, darker in proportion.

Yellow Wing Grey Green — This variety conforms to the standard of Yellow Wing Light Green, except that general body colour should be dull mustard green. **Cheek patches:** grey to slate. **Tail:** long feathers, darker in proportion. (It should be noted that there are light, medium and dark shades of Yellow Wing Grey Green.)

Whitewing Skyblue — **Mask:** white. **Cheek patches:** violet. **General body colour:** back, rump, breast, flanks and underparts, pure skyblue approximating to the normal variety. **Wings:** white, as free from markings as possible. **Tail:** long feathers, bluish. (**Note:** Clearwings showing opaline characteristics should be shown in the A.O.C. or V class.)

Whitewing Cobalt — As above but with a cobalt body colour. **Tail:** long feathers, darker in proportion.

Whitewing Mauve — As above but with a mauve body colour. **Tail:** long feathers, darker in proportion.

Whitewing Violet — As above but with a violet body colour. **Tail:** long feathers, darker in proportion.

Whitewing Grey — As above but with a grey body colour. **Cheek patches:** grey-blue. **Tail:** long feathers, grey. (It should be noted that there are light, medium and dark shades of Whitewing Grey.)

Fallow Light Green — Mask: yellow, ornamented by six evenly spaced large round brown throat spots, the outer two being partially covered at the base by cheek patches. **Cheek patches:** violet. **General body colour:** back, rump, breast, flanks and underparts yellowish green. **Markings:** on cheeks, back of head, neck and wings, medium brown on a yellow ground. **Eyes:** red or plum. **Tail:** long feathers, bluish grey.

Fallow Dark Green — As above but with a light laurel green body colour. **Tail:** long feathers, darker in proportion.

Fallow Olive Green — As above but with a light mustard olive green body colour. **Tail:** long feathers, darker in proportion.

Fallow Grey Green — As above but with a dull mustard green body colour. **Cheek patches:** grey to slate. **Tail:** long feathers, darker in proportion. (It should be noted that there are light, medium and dark shades of Fallow Grey Green.)

Fallow Skyblue — Mask: white, ornamented by six evenly spaced large round brown throat spots, the outer two being partially covered at the base by cheek patches. **Cheek patches:** violet. **General body colour:** back, rump, breast, flanks and underparts, pale skyblue. **Markings:** on cheeks, back of head, neck and wings, medium brown on a white ground. **Eyes:** red or plum. **Tail:** long feathers, bluish grey.

Fallow Cobalt — As above but with a warm cobalt body colour. **Tail:** long feathers, darker in proportion.

Fallow Mauve — As above but with a pale mauve body colour of a pinkish tone. **Tail:** long feathers, darker in proportion.

Fallow Grey — As above but with a pale grey body colour. **Cheek patches:** grey to slate. **Tail:** long feathers, darker in proportion. (It should be noted that there are light, medium and dark shades of Fallow Grey.) English and German forms are recognised: the German form having a white iris ring round the eye, the English form has none.

Lutino — Buttercup yellow throughout. **Eyes:** clear red. **Cheek patches:** silvery white. **Tail:** long feathers and primaries yellowish white.

Albino — White throughout. **Eyes:** clear red.

Yellow Face — All varieties in the blue series except pieds. **Mask:** yellow only, otherwise exactly as the corresponding normal variety. **Note:** yellow marked feathers in tail permissible.

Dominant Pied Light Green — Mask: buttercup yellow of an even tone, ornamented by six evenly spaced and clearly defined large round black throat spots, the outer two being partially covered at the base by cheek patches. **Cheek patches:** violet. **General body colour:** as the normal light green variety but broken with irregular patches of clear buttercup yellow or with a clear yellow band approximately $\frac{1}{2}$ inch (13 mm) wide round its middle just above the thighs. An all yellow or normal green coloured body should be penalized. Head patch is optional. (**Note:** all other things being equal, preference to be given, in accordance with the scale of show points, to birds showing the band.) **Wings:** colour and markings as the normal light green but having irregular patches of clear buttercup yellow or with part of the wing edges to shoulder butt clear yellow on an otherwise normal marked wing. Completely clear wings should be penalised. Wing markings may be grizzled in appearance. All visible flight feathers should be clear yellow but odd dark flight feathers are not faults. **Tail:** the two long tail feathers may be clear yellow, marked or normal blue–

71

black in colour. **Cere:** similar to that of the normal light green or a mixture of normal colour and fleshy pink. **Eyes:** dark with light iris ring. **Beak:** normal horn colour. **Feet and legs:** blue mottled as the normal light green, fleshy pink or a mixture of both.

Dominant Pied Dark Green — As above but with a general body colour as for normal Dark Green.

Dominant Pied Olive Green — As above but with general body colour as for normal Olive Green.

Dominant Pied Grey Green — As above but with general body colour as for normal Grey Green. **Cheek patches:** grey-blue to slate. (It should be noted that there are light, medium and dark shades of Dominant Pied Grey Green.)

Dominant Pied Skyblue — **Mask:** white, ornamented by six evenly spaced and clearly defined large round black throat spots, the outer two being partially covered at the base by cheek patches. **Cheek patches:** violet. **General body colour:** as the normal Skyblue variety but broken with irregular patches of white or with a clear white band approximately ½ inch (13 mm) wide round its middle just above the thighs. An all white or normal blue coloured body should be penalised. Head-patch is optional. (**Note:** all other things being equal, preference to be given, in accordance with the scale of show points, to birds showing the band.) **Wings:** colour and markings as the normal Skyblue but having irregular patches of clear white or with part of the wing edges to shoulder butt clear white on an otherwise normal marked wing. Completely clear wings should be penalised. Wing markings may be grizzled in appearance. All visible flight feathers should be clear white, but odd dark feathers are not faults. **Tail:** the two long tail feathers may be clear white, marked or normal blue-black in colour. **Cere:** similar to that of normal Skyblue or a mixture of normal colour and fleshy pink. **Eyes:** dark with light iris ring. **Beak:** normal horn colour. **Feet and legs:** blue mottled as the normal Skyblue, fleshy pink or a mixture of both.

Dominant Pied Cobalt — As above but with general body colour as for normal Cobalt.

Dominant Pied Mauve — As above but with general body colour as for normal Mauve.

Dominant Pied Violet — As above but with general body colour as for normal Violet.

Dominant Pied Grey — As above but with general body colour as for normal Grey. **Cheek patches:** grey-blue or slate. (It should be noted that there are light, medium and dark shades of Dominant Pied Grey.) **Note:** an Opaline, Yellow Face and Cinnamon form of Dominant Pied is recognised, but these should be shown in the Dominant Pied Classes.

Clearflight Light Green — **Mask:** buttercup yellow of an even colour ornamented by six evenly spaced clearly defined large round black throat spots, the outer two being partially covered at the base by the cheek patches. **Cheek patches:** violet. **General body colour:** as the normal Light Green with the exception of one small patch approximately ½ inch (13 mm) by ⅝ inch (15 mm) of clear buttercup yellow at the back of the head. Slight collar or extension of the bib, while undesirable, will not be penalised. **Wings:** colour and markings as the normal Light Green but with seven visible flight feathers of clear yellow. Dark flights constitute a fault. **Tail:** the two long feathers should be clear yellow, dark tail feathers are a fault. **Cere:** similar to that of normal Light Green. **Eyes:** dark with light iris ring. **Beak:** normal horn colour. **Feet and legs:** mottled or flesh coloured.

Clearflight Dark Green — As above but with general body colour as for normal Dark Green.

Clearflight Olive Green — As above but with general body colour as for normal Olive Green.

Clearflight Grey Green — As above but with general body colour as for normal Grey Green. **Cheek patches:** grey-blue or slate. (It should be noted that there are light, medium and dark shades of Pied (Clear Flighted) Grey Green.)

Clearflight Skyblue — **Mask:** white, ornamented by six evenly spaced clearly defined large round black throat spots, the outer two being partially covered at the base by cheek patches. **Cheek patches:** violet. **General body colour:** as the normal Skyblue with the exception of one small patch approximately $\frac{1}{2}$ inch (13 mm) by $\frac{5}{8}$ inch (15 mm) of pure white at the back of the head. Slight collar or extension of bib, while undesirable, will not penalise. **Wings:** as normal Skyblue but with seven visible flight feathers of pure white. Dark flights constitute a fault. **Tail:** the two, long feathers should be pure white, marked or dark tail feathers are a fault. **Cere:** similar to that of normal Skyblue. **Eyes:** dark with light iris ring. **Beak:** normal horn colour. **Feet and Legs:** bluish mottled or flesh colour.

Clearflight Cobalt — As above but with general body colour as for normal Cobalt.

Clearflight Mauve — As above but with general body colour as for normal Mauve.

Clearflight Violet — As above but with general body colour as for normal Violet.

Clearflight Grey — As above but with general body colour as for normal Grey. **Cheek patches:** grey-blue to slate. (It should be noted that there are light, medium and dark shades of Clearflight Grey.) **Note:** Opaline, Yellow-Face and Cinnamon forms of Clearflights are recognised but these should only be shown in clearflight classes. The non-head spot type of Clearflight (described as Australian) with full body colour is recognised and should be exhibited in Clearflight classes where these are provided.

Dark Eyed Clear Yellow — **Cheek patches:** silvery white. **General body colour:** pure yellow throughout and free from any odd green feathers or green suffusion. **Wings:** pure yellow throughout, free from black of grizzled tickings or green suffusion. All flight feathers paler yellow than rump colour. **Tail:** as the flight feathers. **Cere:** fleshy pink in colour as in Lutinos. **Eyes:** dark without any light iris rings. **Beak:** orange coloured. **Feet and legs:** fleshy pink. **Note:** the actual body colour varies in depth according to the genetic makeup, i.e. whether light, dark or olive green, etc.

Dark Eyed Clear White — As above but with white body colour and free from any blue suffusion or odd blue feathers. **Flights and tail:** white. **Cere:** fleshy pink in colour as in albinos. (**Note:** a dominant form is also recognised having normal cere, eyes, beak, feet and legs, which may be exhibited with the above mentioned types of Dark Eyed Yellow and/or Whites where separate classes are scheduled for this variety. A yellow-faced form of dark eyed clear is also recognised but should only be shown in Dark-eyed Clear classes.)

Recessive Pied Light Green — **Mask:** buttercup yellow of an even tone. **Throat spots:** as the normal Light Green variety; may be present from one to full number. **Cheek patches:** violet, silvery white or a mixture of both. **General body colour:** irregular patches of clear buttercup yellow and bright grass green with the latter mainly on the lower chest, rump and underparts. Zebra markings on the top of the head and around the eyes are not faults. **Wings:** black undulations or polka dot markings should not cover more than 15 to 20 per cent of total area. All visible flight feathers should be clear yellow but odd dark flight feathers are not faults. **Cere:** fleshy pink in colour as in Lutinos. **Eyes:** dark without any light iris ring. **Beak:** orange coloured. **Feet and legs:** fleshy pink.

73

Recessive Pied Dark Green — As above with a yellow and dark green body colour.

Recessive Pied Olive Green — As above but with a yellow and olive green body colour.

Recessive Pied Grey Green — As above but with a yellow and grey-green body colour. **Cheek patches:** grey-blue or slate, or a mixture of both. (It should be noted that there are light, medium and dark shades of Recessive Pied Grey-Green.)

Recessive Pied Skyblue — **Mask:** white. **Throat spots:** as the normal Skyblue variety: may be present from one to a full number. **Cheek patches:** violet, silvery white or a mixture of both. **General body colour:** irregular patches of white and bright skyblue with the latter mainly on the lower chest, rump and underparts. Zebra markings on top of head and around the eyes are not faults. **Wings:** black undulations or polka dot markings should not cover more than fifteen to twenty per cent of total area. All visible flight feathers should be white, but odd dark flight feathers are not faults. **Cere:** fleshy pink in colour as in Albinos. **Eyes:** dark without any light iris ring. **Beak:** orange coloured. **Feet and legs:** fleshy pink.

Recessive Pied Cobalt — As above but with a white and cobalt body colour.

Recessive Pied Mauve: — As above but with a white and mauve body colour.

Recessive Pied Violet — As above but with a white and violet body colour.

Recessive Pied Grey — As above but with a white and grey body colour. **Cheek patches:** grey-blue or slate, or a mixture of both. (It should be noted that there are light, medium and dark forms of Recessive Pied Grey.) **Note:** Opaline, Yellow-Face and Cinnamon forms of Recessive Pied are recognised but these should be shown only in Recessive Pied Classes.

Lacewing Yellow — **Mask:** yellow, ornamented by six evenly spaced large round cinnamon throat spots, the outer two being partially covered at the base by cheek patches. **Cheek patches:** pale violet. **General body colour:** back, rump, breast, flanks and underparts, yellow. **Markings:** on cheeks, back of head, neck, mantle and wings, cinnamon brown on a yellow ground. **Eyes:** clear with light iris rings. **Tail:** long feathers, cinnamon brown. **Note:** the depth of yellow in the body colour, etc., varies according to the normal counterpart being masked by the lacewing character, i.e. the richest yellow is carried by the lacewing olive green and the lighter by the Lacewing Light Green.

Lacewing White — **Mask:** white, ornamented by six evenly spaced large round cinnamon throat spots, the outer two being partially covered at the base by cheek patches. **Cheek patches:** pale violet. **General body colour:** back, rump, breast, flanks and underparts, white. **Markings:** on cheeks, back of head, neck, mantle and wings, cinnamon brown on a white ground. **Eyes:** clear red with light iris rings. **Tail:** long feathers, cinnamon brown. **Note:** the shade of white of the body colour, etc. varies only slightly in tone according to the normal counterpart being masked by the lacewing character. (A yellow-faced form is recognised. Where no classes are scheduled for this variety it should be shown in **Any Other Colour** classes.)

INTERPRETATION OF STANDARDS

We now have the full official picture of what constitutes the ideal Budgerigar, whatever its colour may be. No matter what the *standard* may state, however, most of the points on it are open to interpretation. For example, spots, according to the *standard*, should be *six evenly spaced large round throat spots*, but one may well ask the question how large is large? Does the *standard* refer to spots being large in relation to a five

74

pence piece, or to a pin head? Clearly these are exaggerations, but I am sure the reader will take the point. Perhaps I should make it clear that no disrespect is intended here to the gentlemen of **The Budgerigar Society** who drew up the *standards*. It is used only as a means of illustrating the point.

Similarly, *Neck To be short and wide when viewed from either side or front.* How short? 1 inch, ½ inch, and how wide? Wide in relation to the head or the shoulder? Fortunately, **The Budgerigar Society** has also illustrated its *standard* with an outline reproduction of the ideal bird, and it is this reproduction, in conjunction with the *standard*, which judges use to evaluate birds. Most breeders have this drawing pinned up in their bird rooms, and have probably spent hours looking at it and fixing a mental picture of it in their minds. I strongly advise the beginner in particular to carry out the same exercise.

There are a number of points which should be especially noted about the ideal bird. Firstly, beginning at the top of the cere — which is the bulge at the top of the beak in which the nostrils are situated — note how the line of the front of the skull swings forward away from the face before starting to curve upward into an almost perfect semi-circle over the top of the head and down to the top of the neck, the back skull. Note also the line from the back skull to the top of the shoulder, which should be as straight as possible, as should the continuing line of the back to the root of the tail. The tail itself should curve very slightly upward, though not excessively so. Note the line of the draw, the part from behind the thigh to the root of the tail and sweeping back through the top of the thigh to a deep well curved chest with good depth from its deepest point to the shoulder. Note then the inward curve of the chest back toward the beak, and the beak itself set neatly into the face. Note the mask, deep and wide when viewed from the front, and the spots, evenly spaced and large in comparison to the remainder of the mask as the *standard* suggests. Lastly, note the position of the eye and its relation to the head, and note that it is almost precisely in the centre, and the cheek patches, covering the outermost spot, again, as the *standard* suggests.

Having examined the outline of the bird, look at the markings and see how even and clearly defined they are. Note also the line of the wing carried in the ideal with the tips almost touching above the root of the tail and carried along the line of the body. Note the angle on the perch with the foot in an almost straight line beneath the eye, and finally, note the alertness in that stance. Looking at the outline, and examining each point as indicated here, should enable the fancier to fix his own picture of the bird firmly, but there are other points which are not so apparent in the outline drawings of the ideal.

75

In the ideal budgerigar we have a bird standing at the correct angle of thirty degrees from the vertical, with neatly fitting and well tucked-in beak, and good forward rise and upward lift of skull sweeping over to an excellent back-line. The eye is well placed, alert and fearless, and there is a good deep mask with well rounded and evenly spaced spots set not too high on the mask. The markings fall back from the eye to give that greatly desired free-from-ticking look which is so important. Excellent width of face is clearly indicated as is thickness of neck. The breast-line is right, conveying just enough depth to give a proper balance overall. Nicely cut away between the legs, this bird stands just sufficiently high above the perch. The wings are cushioned neatly on the body giving an uninterrupted line from head to tip of tail.

Figure 6.2 The Budgerigar Society Ideal — Three-Quarter View *Courtesy* The Budgerigar Society

From the front, the head should also be round in an almost perfect semi-circle from brow to brow. One of the most difficult features to achieve in breeding Budgerigars is the desired circular head, and a great many birds are bred with heads which are said to 'cut off' at the back skull giving an elongated appearance, or which are said to be 'nipped in at the head' which is generally taken to imply that the skull above the eye, instead of widening out as it should, has the appearance more of a conical shape with the point of the cone flattened.

The mask, likewise, when viewed from the front should be deep and wide, and clearly defined over the chest. Again, ideally, it should have that perfect semi-circle showing off the depth and width of the chest. The beak should not be too wide, in the same way that it should not protrude when viewed from the side, but should be neat and commensurate in size with the rest of the face.

The chest should have an equally deep, wide and rounded appearance from the front as from the side and should show the even colour as outlined in the *standard*, with no patchiness.

FAULTS WHICH SHOULD BE AVOIDED

Having now gained a clear picture of what is required in a Budgerigar needed for the purpose of producing exhibition stock, let us now consider the more common faults, and those which are undesirable in the parent birds. Remember, however, that if the ideal bird is bred, it will certainly not be for sale at any price, and that in the beginning, the newcomer to the fancy will have to make some compromise. A start will have to be made with birds which do carry faults, but, of course, the fewer there are in the initial stock, the better.

Head

Avoid birds with 'nipped in' heads as described earlier. This is an extremely difficult fault to breed out. Avoid birds lacking in a good sweep of back skull. The fault known as 'cut off' is very common, and, again, is very difficult to breed out. Birds with what is termed 'a bifurcated mask' should also be avoided. This is usually caused by over-feathering, which we will discuss later, and is usually indicative of a bird which, while appearing to possess a good head, may really have a small head and a lot of feather. Similar remarks apply to the chests of many birds.

Birds with poor spots should be avoided if possible, but this particular fault is not so difficult to breed out as are the others relating to the shape of the head. Neither, for that matter is the bifurcated mask or chest, but we will come to those particular problems later. It may also be better to avoid birds which have ticked or barred heads. The head should be a clean colour as described in the *standard*, but it should be pointed out that birds carrying head ticking may not necessarily pass this fault on to their young.

A point of which the beginner should be made aware on the subject of head quality is that, in general terms, a cock with a good head will always have a better head than a hen. The cock Budgerigar has, as a general rule, more back skull than has a hen, giving a higher curve to the head as a whole, and it should be remembered that a hen which appears to be lacking back skull in comparison to a cock, may still be a good headed hen.

Neck

As with the 'nipped in' head, birds which show a 'nipped in' neck, either from front or side view, should certainly be avoided. Although the *standard* describes the neck of the ideal Budgerigar, the neck as such should be invisible, in the sense that it should run in an unbroken line from shoulder to head from whatever angle the bird is viewed. A 'nipped in' neck is regarded as a very bad fault, giving the bird the appearance of small headedness, clearly not in line with the *standard*.

Shoulders

Continuing down the back of the bird, avoid birds with humped shoulders, which will completely spoil the almost straight line of the back. Similarly, birds are often seen with a lift of the back line just before the root of the tail. This fault completely spoils the wing carriage.

Chest

Birds with narrow chest should be avoided. The bodily faults are the most difficult to breed out, and a slender narrow bird is useless for the breeding of exhibition stock. Size, as we have seen, is all important, and is the most difficult attribute to set into a stud. Birds with faults in any aspect of size should be avoided.

Wings

Birds with faulty wing carriage, either the so called 'scissored wings', that is, birds which carry the wings too high above the body causing the ends of the primary flights to cross, or dropped wings, carrying the wings downward and away from the body, should also be avoided. Some fanciers still believe in what is termed the 'averaging out theory', which states that if a bird with scissored wings is mated to a bird with dropped wings, then the progeny will have a normal wing carriage. Since, as we shall see, the science of genetics simply does not work in that manner, the beginner should ignore such advice.

Tail

Avoid birds which have a dropped tail. This, apart from being a major fault, not only spoils the appearance of the bird because of the particular fault, but will also spoil the wing carriage, causing the scissor wing effect.

Feet

Look closely at the feet and make sure they have the required number of toes and nails and having paid attention to all of these points, then have a good look at the overall bird.

Overall Appearance

Note the colour of the bird and make sure that it is deep, and above all, even. Unevenness is not too bad a fault in a single bird, but obviously it is better to avoid it if possible. Look at the position of the bird in a show cage and ask whether it is standing at the correct angle, fearlessly and brightly. Does it appear to be completely at ease, or is it down on the floor of the cage, perhaps with its head under the drinker, a favourite position for birds which are afraid of show cages. There is a theory, which I believe to be true, that 'showmanship' can be bred into a stud, and it is widely held that birds which have come from show stock are much easier to train for the show bench and much less likely to mis-behave at the show than those which come from parents not showing these attributes.

Above all, look at the general **condition** of the bird. If it sits fluffed out on its perch, possibly hugging the wall of the flight or stock cage, then the bird is probably suffering from some disorder. Similarly, a bird which sits somewhat dejectedly on its perch with its tail rising and falling rapidly in a pumping action is equally certainly ill. There are other obvious signs of illness which will be apparent even if the particular disease is not affecting the bird one intends to buy.

Look closely at the vents of the birds. If they appear to be more soiled than they should, especially if the vent appears greenish in colour, then have nothing to do with any bird from that cage or flight. Examine the droppings on the floor, if they are loose and greenish or yellowish in colour, then similar remarks apply. Birds breathing more quickly than normally should also be avoided, but for the most part, the most apparent signs of illness are the bird with its feathers fluffed out and that which pumps its tail up and down rhythmically.

Another good pointer is the state of the bird room. If the room is untidy, then that is of little consequence. If it is dirty, however, then that is an entirely different matter: have nothing to do with it or the seller and leave without making a purchase as politely as possible. A dirty bird room is a sure sign that the owner is either a very bad manager, or has insufficient time to care for his stock correctly. Either way, birds purchased from such an establishment are probably not in the best of health and will almost certainly not be in the high state of general health required for breeding.

Having described the ideal bird, the good points desirable and the bad points to be avoided, there remains one further factor which should be taken into consideration before the fancier decides on the type of bird to be used to form the foundation of the stud. This is feather quality.

YELLOW AND BUFF FEATHER

The beginner, in particular, should understand clearly that there are two distinct types of feather, namely the yellow and the buff. Although the words used are descriptive of colours, the terms are used to describe the type of feather and have no relation to colour. The yellow feather is a long fine and silky feather, and the buff is a broader, coarser and much larger structure with white or silvery fringes, known as 'frosting' for obvious reasons.

The continued mating of a yellow feathered bird to others of similar feathering will produce long flighted birds, that is, birds with wings longer than they should be, a very bad fault, and, further, which will have an elongated appearance, the usual term for which is 'snaky'.

Conversely, the continual mating of a buff feathered bird to ones with similar feathering will produce birds with the bifurcated masks and chests previously mentioned. In addition birds will be produced which, although they may appear large, will be, as fanciers term it, 'birds of no substance', or, to put the situation another way, they will be small in themselves, but will carry large amounts of feather giving the appearance of being large birds. Attempts to fool the judges by continually breeding buff to buff have often been made, but I suspect that they have rarely, if ever, succeeded. Any experienced judge will very quickly recognise such a bird for what it is rather than what it appears to be and will act accordingly, usually by placing it last in the class!

AGE OF THE PAIR

It is usually accepted by experienced breeders that, although the age of the breeding pairs is not important — provided that they are not too old for breeding — it is better when making a start to what one hopes is a true breeding line to have a young hen in her first breeding season, and an adult cock. The reason being that a cock will go on breeding effectively, so far as the quality of the young is concerned, for perhaps two seasons more than the hen, and attention should be paid to this point when the initial breeding stock is being chosen.

DOUBLE FAULTS

Because of factors involved in genetic inheritance which will be discussed later, the beginner should be made aware that under no circumstances should two birds be paired together which carry the same fault. This will only compound that fault in the offspring and will establish it into the line, a highly undesirable state of affairs. Such pairings must, therefore, be avoided.

The beginner purchasing stock for the first time is advised to put colour only secondary to the size, type and so on of the birds he is intending to buy. An old fancier friend was often heard to remark, 'if it's a good bird it will win no matter what colour it is', and in the main, I believe this to be true. Obviously some of the more recent additions to the colour scale, the pieds and so on, have not yet reached the standards required to beat some of the older, and therefore, better established colours, the greens, blues and more normal colours. If the fancier sticks to the older varieties, however, then the remark holds good. At any event, colour is not important at this stage, because in the first two or three seasons the newcomer to the fancy will see many birds on the show benches which he has not seen before, and which he may wish to specialise in later.

A good compromise is to start with perhaps four pairs of birds, with one normal and one opaline in each pair. If, for example, there is a pair of greys, a pair of blues and two pairs of greens, some of which may be split for other colours, then the first year breeder is probably assured of having several colours which he can then enter at the shows, giving him a better chance in more classes than if he bred only from one colour.

Throughout all of this, however, I will repeat what I said at the beginning of this chapter. Remember that the best advice which can be given is that a newcomer should join the local society, make certain that the exhibitor chosen as a supplier is well established and experienced and that he is respected by his fellow fanciers. The beginner can do no better than to put himself in the hands of such a person.

One final point concerns the time of year. In October, the experienced fanciers have probably decided which of their stock they wish to keep and which they intend to sell. Obviously the sooner purchases are made the better, because the choice will be greater and the better birds will not have been sold. Almost always, there are 'borderline cases' in any birdroom, birds which the fancier finds difficulty in assessing for one reason or another. This type of bird is probably the real bargain, and is the type which should be sought.

CHAPTER 7

THE BREEDING SEASON

There is one prime rule for the start of the breeding season, 'always pair best to best', and this rule holds true especially for the beginner. If, as has been suggested, the beginner has found a reputable supplier, then he will be well aware which of his birds should be paired to which mate. If for any reason he is not sure, then he is strongly advised to seek the advice of a more experienced fancier.

The decision on which cock is to be paired to which hen should be made by the end of October at the latest if early breeding is the aim. Most experienced fanciers aim at pairing their birds up and having young chicks in the nest very early in January in order that their young stock can be ready for the early shows in June and July: this has now reached what I believe to be ridiculous proportions, because some fanciers have young birds in the nest boxes early in November. Since a young chick must be closed rung when it is five days old, and is too old by the end of seven days, such fanciers are ringing their chicks as proof of their own breeding, using rings left over from the previous breeding season. Since the object of early breeding is to have current year bred birds ready for the early shows, and since birds cannot be shown in the breeders classes without a current year closed ring, the logic of that exercise defeats me completely. The closed rings which are issued each year by **The Budgerigar Society** and which bear the code number of the member concerned, are issued on January 1st. If the chicks have been bred early, or perhaps one might say too early, then the chicks must not be more than four days old at the extreme, allowing for postal delays, and if there is a delay of only three days, then the chicks will be too old for ringing by the time the rings arrive.

Although fanciers are now carrying on the practice of what one can only term ludicrously early breeding, it would be much fairer to say of

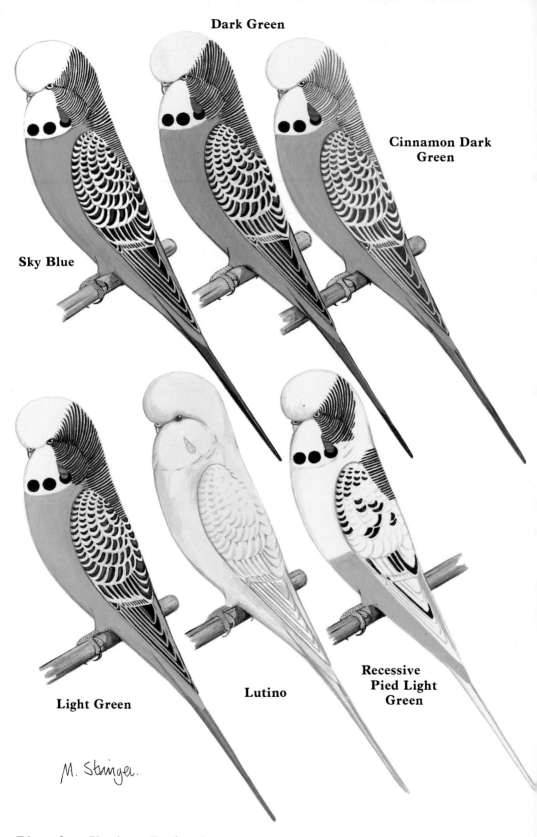

Dark Green

Cinnamon Dark Green

Sky Blue

Light Green

Lutino

Recessive Pied Light Green

M. Stringer.

Plate 1 — Various Budgerigars.

the fancy as a whole that most breeders aim to have chicks in the nest at the end of the second week in January. In order to do that, work must be started much earlier.

BRINGING INTO BREEDING CONDITION

The birds will certainly not be in a natural breeding condition at the time at which the fancier wishes them to breed, and, therefore, artificial means of bringing that about must be found. This is achieved with the aid of artificial heat, and especially light. At the beginning of November there are roughly nine hours of daylight. This is not sufficient for Budgerigar breeding purposes, and that time must be extended if the birds are to be in condition at the appropriate time.

In the second week in November, the time is extended by two hours and should be then extended by one hour each week until the birds have fourteen hours of light each day, that is, fourteen hours in all of artificial plus natural daylight combined. If the suggestion presented earlier is followed, i.e. that the artificial light is provided at the beginning of the day, rather than at the end, this means turning on the aviary lights at 2.00 a.m., setting them to turn off at around 8.00 a.m. when it is fully daylight. This again, in my view, only underlines the somewhat less than natural conditions with which the birds are expected to deal, simply because of the whims of fanciers putting on shows relatively early in the year.

The reason for the fourteen hours of daylight (or perhaps light would be a better word), is that when Budgerigar chicks are very small, they must be fed at very frequent intervals with only a little food at any one feed being given. Some fanciers employ the use of small nightlights, expecting the hens to feed their chicks by the light of a very dim red or blue bulb — I do not believe that the birds do this as often as many fanciers appear to imagine. It follows that if the young chicks need frequent feeding, but the parents cannot carry out their duties because of a lack of light, the result will be the starvation of the chicks in the nest. Even if they do not actually starve to death, their growth will certainly be retarded, thus defeating the object of the exercise. The reason for this last, is that the rate of growth of a Budgerigar chick must almost be seen to be believed. So rapidly do the young birds grow that at times they appear almost to swell before one's eyes. Clearly, they cannot grow at such a rate with an insufficient food intake, especially as we have seen, of the all important protein, and the logical result of all of this is as previously stated; either they will starve to death during the night, or will be stunted in their growth. Either way, unless the daylight hours are extended to fourteen by artificial means, the whole object of early breeding has been defeated before it has even started and few if any of the birds produced will be of any practical use either for showing or for inclusion in the breeding season the following year.

By this time, the reader will no doubt gather that I am not in favour of early breeding. It is often said that birds should be kept in conditions as close to nature as possible, but some of the same people who advocate this are the very people who are carrying out these unnatural practices!

It may well be that the reader disagrees with these comments, and wishes to carry out early breeding regardless. If so, then I wish him well, but I most strongly advise beginners not to begin breeding operations until later, at the end of February. In that case, the remarks concerning the use of artificial light still apply, but the gradual build up to fourteen hours of light need not begin until New Year's Day.

At the same time, the normal weekly supply of soft food should be increased to twice weekly, gradually building until the birds are receiving small amounts four times each week. One teaspoonful for each bird is sufficient for one feed.

Figure 7.1 Hens will become accustomed to having the Nest Box opened, and will leave the Nest quietly so that the Chicks can be examined

84

Added to all of which, the heating should be kept at a constant 50 degrees Fahrenheit (10C), and these combined factors of an increase in heat and the hours of light plus the extra soft food should begin to bring the birds into full breeding condition at the appropriate time. This is a very critical time indeed for the fancier, and it is at this point that a cardinal error may be made, namely, that of pairing the birds when they are not physically or mentally prepared to carry out their parental duties.

Because of individual circumstances, it is unlikely that turning on the bird room lights at 2.00 a.m. as suggested will be convenient. Most people do not reach home after their work until after 5.00 p.m., at which time, in the winter months, it is already dark. This method also means that the birds will have to be attended to before the fancier leaves for work in the morning, which, again, is rather inconvenient, especially if one has a relatively large stud to look after. In those circumstances, the use of a dimmer switch should be employed and set to dim down the lights so that the bird room is in darkness at 10.00 p.m.

Some dimmer switches dim the lights automatically, and there are others which must be operated manually. Since the difference in price between the two is not great, and one needs this type of appliance in any event, then I suggest the use of the automatic type.

In this respect, the fancier will have to work out a time scale to suit himself. Remember that the aim is to provide fourteen hours of light. **When** that light is provided is not important, it is the **length** of time which is the governing factor.

BREEDING CONDITION

Having brought the birds into breeding condition by judicious use of artificial light and heat and going to the trouble to prepare soft food in increasing quantities each week, many fanciers, newcomers and champions alike, frequently make the mistake of pairing birds too early

When Budgerigars are in full breeding condition the ceres become darker and brighter in colour, brown in the case of the hen, and bright blue in the case of the cock. Frequently, this state of affairs may be achieved, but these signs in themselves are not necessarily indications that the bird in question is ready and prepared to go to nest. In conjunction with the condition of the cere, the bird will be tighter in feather than is normally the case, and becomes restless. Cocks and hens begin to call constantly to each other and display signs of readiness to mate.

In the case of the cocks, they will increase their normal habit of banging their beaks on the perches and sides of the cages, and will begin to 'feed' the bars of the cage fronts with regurgitated food.

Figure 7.2 A Bird Room set up for the start of the Breeding Season. Note that all of the Nest Boxes are outside the cages, therefore allowing a single cage to be used for each pair

Meanwhile, the hens will carry on in a similar manner and will begin to squat on their perches and call constantly to the cocks. Not until both birds are seen to be displaying all of these characteristics should they be placed together in the same cage.

It should also be pointed out that there is no point at all in putting a pair together because one is obviously ready for breeding while the other is perhaps showing only the dark cere on the assumption that one will force the other to mate and to nest. Nothing could be further from the truth, but it is on such assumptions that many mistakes are made. I can quite appreciate the fancier wishing to see the outcome of careful selection, and perhaps coupled with it the results of perhaps three or four seasons' work, but there is only one word which applies here if there is the slightest doubt: **wait**. If one of the pair is not ready, then no matter how many seasons the fancier has waited for this one pairing, the result will be disastrous. If the cock is not ready then the eggs may well be infertile. If the hen is not ready then there will be no eggs and if there are, these too will probably be infertile. It cannot be stressed too strongly that **only** when both cock and hen are in full condition will they attempt to mate and tend their young.

PREPARING THE BREEDING CAGE

No special preparations should be necessary so far as the cleanliness of the cage itself is concerned. Cages and feeding utensils should be kept scrupulously clean at all times, whether breeding is going on or not, but if there is any doubt, then give the cage an extra wash with disinfectant two days before the birds are introduced to each other.

Also at this time, the normally round perches should be exchanged for square ones. This will enable the hen to grip the perch much tighter during mating, and will help to ensure that a correct mating takes place. Also make certain that the perches are very firmly fixed. When the cage is being prepared, and after it has been well washed down, give a good spray with an antimite solution, most especially in the corners. After the birds have begun their breeding cycle, they should be disturbed as little as possible, and the normal cleaning routine is not carried out during this period apart from what is absolutely necessary. It is very important, therefore, that special attention should be given at this point.

NEST BOXES

Nest boxes in which the pair are comfortably able to rear their chicks will also be needed at this stage, and there are several types. Regardless of the type of nest box being used, the size is roughly the same at about

Figure 7.3 The Constituent parts of a Nest Box

nine inches long, six inches wide and seven inches high (22.86 cm x 15.24 cm x 17.78 cm). In the bottom, a concave floor is fitted, which is removable. This consists of a piece of wood about one inch (2.54 cm) thick, in one end of which a depression about four inches (10.61 cm) in diameter and $\frac{5}{8}$ inch (1.59 cm) deep has been hollowed out. The reason for using such a nest is that in the wild, Budgerigars make their nests in hollow trees, making a 'scrape' among the dead bark inside, and this is about as close as the fancier can come to recreating those conditions.

If the fancier is considering making his own nest boxes, and I suggest that he does, the outside of the box should be made as close as possible to the dimensions of the concave. There should be no gap between the edges of the concave and the sides of the box. If there are, then the young chicks might easily trap their feet and legs with possible disastrous results. To guard against this type of accident, fanciers place sawdust into the small gaps which are bound to exist. It is a practical impossibility to make the concave a precise fit because if the dimensions of the box and the concave are exactly the same, then the concave would not fit and must, therefore, be at least a tiny fraction smaller.

Desk Type Nest Box

Many fanciers used nest boxes known as the desk type, and indeed, many do today. This type of box, as the name suggests, is shaped like the top of a desk. The lid is hinged roughly half way along the box, and the entrance hole, which should be $2\frac{1}{8}$ inch (5.40 cm) in diameter is on top of the box in the solid portion. The advantage of this type of box is that there is no danger of the chicks falling out or eggs being broken, but its disadvantage is that it has to be moved outside the cage for purposes of cleaning or examining eggs or chicks.

Another type of nest box in popular use and the type most usually found in the pet shops, is the type with a sliding end. This type has a glass slide toward the open end of the box, and a solid wooden slide over that. The advantage of this type is that the interior of the nest box can be seen without disturbing it, but the disadvantage is that it will have to be removed from its position on the wall of the cage for this purpose.

Yet another type favoured by some fanciers is the drawer type. The drawer is constructed so that it can be withdrawn complete with the contents of the nest box but this type also has its disadvantages. If the drawer is withdrawn and an egg or a chick has found its way to the edge of the concave block, away from the concave itself, it may well fall and be injured; an egg, of course, would be broken.

None of these types can really be recommended for the reasons stated, and the type I would recommend, and that which I believe is now more widely used than any other, certainly by experienced fanciers, is a simple rectangular box, with a hinged top and the entrance hole in the end furthest away from the concave. Under the entrance hole, a piece of $\frac{5}{8}$ inch (1.59 cm) round dowel about two inches (5.08 cm) long is installed to give the hen easy access, the hole being $2\frac{1}{8}$ inch in diameter as already stated.

This type of box has several advantages, not the least of which is its positioning. Instead of putting the box inside the cage, as was the practice in years gone by, the box is fastened to the top corner of the cage front, the wires being removed so that the full width of the entrance hole is available to the hen. In that position, and with its hinged top, the box can be examined very easily indeed and what is perhaps more important, without fear of chicks or eggs dropping from the concave to the floor of the bird room. The top should be hinged in such a manner that it will fold all the way back down the side of the box, thus avoiding the possibility of its dropping back and perhaps injuring a chick when it is being removed. Perhaps the most useful attribute of this type of nest box is the fact that by fixing it to the outside of the cage, a single cage is then large enough for breeding purposes, thus releasing other single cages for use as stock cages for the young chicks when they are taken away from their parents.

Another advantage of this type of box is that the entrance hole faces into the cage, away from the windows and gives more privacy to the hen. If this method of providing nest boxes is used, care must be taken to make absolutely certain that the box is fixed very securely, and the best method of achieving this end is to place a thin lath of wood, the same length as the width of the nest box with two small holes, one at each end, inside the cage bars. Two small $\frac{1}{4}$ inch (0.64 cm) bolts can then be pushed through the holes and through corresponding holes in the end of the box and tightened. This will ensure that the box cannot be knocked to the floor if the fancier should accidentally knock into it during feeding or whatever.

The thickness of the material used in construction of nest boxes is important. It is better to use relatively thick timber for the purpose, on the premise that this will help to keep the interior warm. If, as suggested, the concave is $\frac{5}{8}$ inch (1.59 cm) deep, this leaves only $\frac{3}{8}$ inch (0.95 cm) beneath the chicks. Therefore, the thicker the timber, especially beneath the chicks, the better. A good solution to this problem would be to use perhaps $\frac{1}{2}$ inch (1.27 cm) ply for the bottom of the box, and $\frac{3}{8}$ inch (0.95 cm) for the sides and top. There is also the point to consider, that if the bird room is heated, then very thick walled nest

Nest box with sliding wooden door *Courtesy* **Ivy Cottage Bird Farm**

Nest box showing alternative wooden or glass door

Courtesy **Ponderosa**

Figure 7.4 Types of Nest box.

boxes are not necessary since the outside is warm in any event. The nest box should be finished off by drilling a row of small holes (two or three are sufficient) in the end of the nest box facing into the cage. This will allow air to circulate within the box itself. When the nest box is prepared, a little sawdust should be placed in the concave. This will give the eggs a softer bed, and will prevent them from rolling about when the hen turns them, as she will, frequently.

INTRODUCING THE PAIR

There are two distinct schools of thought on this subject, one believing that it is best to put the hen into the cage with the cock, the other that the reverse is the better method. In my view, either method is correct, but I believe it true to say that most fanciers prefer the latter method and put the cock into the cage with the hen.

When the pair are being introduced for the purposes of breeding, a card should be fixed to the front of the breeding cage, recording the number of the ring of both cock and hen, their colour, the date of the first mating, if that is known, and with space for the recording of the laying of each egg and the date when it is expected to hatch, and for other remarks or the recording of any problems which may be encountered, for example, only half the clutch being fertile.

Most breeders stick such cards on the ends of the nest boxes, which makes it a simple matter for a note to be added when the boxes are examined in the routine manner twice daily. The information so recorded can then be transferred to the breeding register which will be used to record the entire breeding season later.

The hens will have been in their breeding cages for at least two weeks before the intended date of pairing, giving them time to settle down to their new surroundings, and to become accustomed to having a different view of the bird room. At the same time that the hen is placed in her breeding cage, the cock will be placed in the adjacent cage and the slide between the two should be withdrawn about a quarter of an inch. This will allow the birds to become aware of each other and will be an aid to their becoming attached.

Two days before the pair are to be introduced, the nest box is placed in position, preferably early in the day to give the hen time to become accustomed to its being there before darkness falls. At this point, some fanciers keep the entrance hole closed on the assumption that this will intrigue the hen and cause her to investigate the interior as soon as it is opened up. Budgerigars being the inquisitive creatures they most certainly are, there can be nothing at all wrong with this theory. Whether it is necessary or not is another matter. Certainly it is a

Figure 7.5   The Pair may be introduced simply by removing the slide between the Cages

method in common use, and the newcomer might like to try half his hens using this method and the other half being supplied with open nest boxes to find out which of the two suits him.

Some breeders may not agree with the method of placing cock and hen in adjacent cages and allowing them to see each other before it is intended they should mate. A method which is widely adopted is to place the hen in the breeding cage two weeks before introducing the cock, and to place the nest box in position two days previously, and to then simply put the cock into the cage with the hen. If the hen has been allowed to settle down in the breeding cage and both she and the cock are in true breeding condition, then mating will probably take place immediately in any event. He will immediately fly to the hen and begin to tap his beak on hers, and possibly begin to feed her. She, assuming that she is amenable to the idea, will squat on the perch with her head lifted in order to be fed, lifting her tail. If this behaviour is observed immediately the cock is introduced, then even if mating is not seen to take place, it is certain that it will do so very soon. All of this, of course, is assuming that the pair are compatible. There is a possibility, however, that they may not be, in which case the hen may well begin to fight with the cock and may even kill him if she is not prevented from so doing.

In order to prevent this, close observation should be kept on the pair for a short time after the cock is introduced. If mating takes place immediately, or the signs are as described above, then the pair may be safely left together. If, however, the hen does reject the cock and begins to fight, he may have to be removed. Sometimes, there will be a little minor altercation between the two, amounting to nothing more than a domestic argument. If that is the case, then, again, the pair may be safely left together.

If, however, the fighting becomes more serious, the chief aggressor will certainly be the hen, and the cock must be removed to his own cage for a few days before another attempt is made to induce the pair to settle down together. All of this sounds very dramatic, but it should be made clear that this is certainly the exception rather than the rule. It is true that one occasionally comes across hens which persistently refuse to mate with any cock, but they are very much the exception. It may also be that the hen for some reason known only to her, takes an instant dislike to her chosen mate, in which case the only solution is to put her with a different cock, but, as already stated, such circumstances are very rarely encountered.

The major cause of such occurrences is that the breeder has not done his job correctly, and that the pair have been introduced before one or the other is ready. In the case of fighting breaking out, this will certainly be the hen. In the case of mating not taking place the cause could be either bird, and if the cock shows no interest in the hen, then it is he who is the cause of the problem. Clearly then, the importance of both birds being in full breeding condition is evident, and vital. This is underlined when one considers that by introducing the cock, then removing him and replacing him later, both birds may become emotionally upset and may never settle down for the remainder of the breeding season. Again, therefore, it must be stressed that full breeding fitness is of the utmost importance.

EGG LAYING

We must assume, however, that all is well and that the pair are compatible and have mated. At that point, the hen will already have entered the nest box and will have become familiar with it. She will gradually begin to spend longer and longer periods in the nest box, at which point the appearance of the first egg is imminent.

After three or four days have passed, and when the hen is in the nest box and the fancier enters the bird room at feeding time, most breeders begin to 'train' the hens to leave the nest boxes. Only, and this must be stressed, **after** the hens have been allowed to become accustomed to the safety of the boxes. When the hen is in the box, the bottom of it should be gently tapped with the finger tips. This will result in the hen leaving the box, so that the lid can be lifted and the interior examined. It really is quite amazing how quickly the hens become accustomed to this, and after only perhaps two days, the hens will accept this calmly, which is the object of the exercise, and will leave the nest box almost immediately. The reason for accustoming the hens to this is so that when there are eggs or chicks in the nest, the hen can be induced to leave the nest box and go into the breeding cage. The lid of the nest box can then be opened without fear of startling the hen and causing her either to panic and injure herself in trying to get back into the cage quickly, or flying out of the top of the box into the open bird room. This would probably necessitate her having to be pursued, resulting in even more panic and the possibility of the desertion of either eggs or chicks.

The first egg will appear at anything between eight to twelve days after the pair have been introduced, and a few days before the event, the hen will be seen to be becoming noticeably more round in the draw, between the back of the thigh and the root of the tail. When she is almost about to lay her first egg, this part of her anatomy will become almost square.

When it is believed that the first egg is about to be laid, the nest boxes should be examined morning and evening for recording purposes. The

Figure 7.6   Nest box with eggs

eggs will be laid on alternate days, that is, for example, Monday, Wednesday, Friday and so on. The usual number is five or six. It has been known for hens to lay nine eggs in a clutch — in those cases, certain actions are called for which will be discussed later in this chapter.

At this stage, some fanciers mark the eggs with a felt tipped pen, one dot for the first, two for the second and so on. In my view, this is unnecessary, since the question of whether one single egg from a clutch is fertile or infertile will be very apparent later, and is purely academic in any event. It can have one advantage, however, in terms of the determination of fertility. If the number of chicks in the nests can be averaged out among the hens so that each hen has the same number of chicks to be reared, preferably four or five at most, then this can be achieved by taking an egg out of one nest and placing it in another. Obviously, there is no point in carrying out this particular exercise if the eggs are infertile, or, indeed, when it is not known whether the eggs are fertile or not.

To overcome this problem, a very useful piece of bird room equipment can be quickly made, which we will term, for want of a better expression, a 'fertility tester'. This consists very simply of a box with a 100 watt bulb inside. In the top of the box, a small oval hole is cut which will allow the egg to rest on top without falling through. When each of the marked eggs has been incubating for seven days, it is placed on the fertility tester, and if it is fertile, small red strands will be clearly seen on the yolk. If the red strands are present, then the egg is fertile. If they are not present, then the egg is infertile. If this practice is to be carried out, then the eggs should be marked as they are laid as described.

The obvious reason is that when the eggs are laid, there is no method of distinguishing one from the other, and if they are not marked then every egg would have to be retested as each new egg reaches the stage at which the signs of its being fertile are evident.

For the benefit of the beginner, there is one point which must be made here, concerning the handling of the eggs. The weakest point in an egg shell is around its middle, where it is extremely delicate. When handling an egg therefore, it should be picked up between the thumb and forefinger at each end, never in the middle. This point should be very carefully noted; otherwise eggs may be broken.

If the eggs are being placed under other pairs in order to average the numbers of chicks, then obviously these must be marked in a different colour to the markings on the eggs of the foster parents. If this is done, the fancier will know which chick belongs to which pair as the eggs hatch. A much safer method, however, is to try to ensure that a bird, for example, from a pair of true breeding blues is placed under a pair of true

97

breeding greens. If this can be achieved then clearly there can be no doubt when the chicks are feathered.

It is also entirely possible, of course, that the egg which the fancier wishes to transfer may be due to hatch on the same day as another egg in the nest to which it is transferred, in which case there is a real problem. The only method which can be adopted then, is for the fancier to keep a very close watch on that particular nest on the day the eggs are due to hatch, and when the fostered chick emerges, to mark it high under the wing, again, using a felt tipped pen. The feathers at this point are the last to develop and, by that time, the fancier will be able to identify the bird because of its colour or markings.

The best method of fostering is to wait until the chicks have hatched under their own parents, and then to mark them under the wing as described before removing them to their foster parents.

Another reason for removing chicks to another nest is that the eggs will hatch on alternate days in the same manner and order that they were laid. If, for example, a hen has five fertile eggs, the chick which was first hatched will be ten days older than the last, and, more importantly, will be considerably larger.

The result of that situation is that the larger siblings will certainly take the lion's share of the food; young birds of around ten days old are voracious creatures, whether Budgerigars or anything else, and will push the smaller chicks down at feeding time, depriving them of food and probably causing their deaths. This, it must be said, is a very unfortunate circumstances, but in my opinion, Budgerigars, being in the wild, would probably take over the entire antipodean continent if nature did not devise some method of restraining them. My belief is that this is her way of ensuring that numbers are kept to reasonable proportions.

EGG BINDING

It is during the process of egg laying that the problem of egg binding may occur. This is a more frequent occurrence in young hens and happens especially with the first egg. There is a belief among fanciers that egg binding is caused mainly through lack of lubrication in the oviduct, but more enlightened fanciers are perfectly well aware that this is not the case. In Budgerigars, there are two main causes of egg binding.

The first is, I believe, peculiar to Budgerigars, although I stand to be corrected upon that point. It is not unknown for the young hen to produce an extra large egg at her first attempt at reproduction. If this occurs, and the hen herself is not too large, then the matter is even further complicated. In fact, the only bird I have ever lost through egg binding was lost through precisely that circumstance. The hen did eventually pass the egg, but died in the process. The egg was perfectly formed, but was very large.

The second cause of egg binding in Budgerigar hens is through the shells being soft, a situation brought about by an under provision of calcium, which is why this substance is especially important for breeding hens, as mentioned earlier. The reasons for a hen being egg bound for the former reason are surely obvious, but the latter may not be quite so easily understood. Because of that, it is perhaps important to describe here the methods by which a hen lays her eggs.

The egg is formed at the top of a channel known as the oviduct, down which it will pass by a natural method little by little and which is called peristaltic action. This acts in the same manner as the method used to pass a ball through a compressible tube by squeezing from behind. Pressure is applied, the ball moves down the tube, and pressure is then reapplied behind the ball. The expulsion of an egg is carried out by the natural movements of the wall of the oviduct in the same manner. If the hen is not supplied with a sufficient intake of calcium, then she will be unable to form the hard shell, and when peristaltic action begins, instead of the pressure of the oviduct compressing the oviduct and forcing the egg down the channel, the soft shell will be compressed and will not move downward.

If such a hen is treated quickly and correctly, however, there is every chance that the egg will be expelled in the normal manner. One point which must be made absolutely clear, however, is that **no attempt** must be made to locate the egg in the oviduct, and **under no circumstances** should any attempt be made to push the egg down the duct by using pressure from behind. This will result in the egg being broken and the inevitable death of the hen.

Any attempt to locate the egg may lead to this result and should be avoided at all costs. As the treatment has nothing to do with the position in the oviduct, the exact location of the egg is completely irrelevant.

The correct treatment for an egg bound hen is to place her in a hospital cage and to raise the temperature to 90 degrees Fahrenheit. This will relax the hen and allow the egg to be expelled normally. When transferring the hen to the hospital cage, a little warm olive oil put around the vent with a small brush may be of assistance, but again, very great care must be taken when handling a hen in this condition. The bird should be held around the chest and neck with the thumb and forefinger and the wings kept to the sides by the ball of the thumb and the little finger. Under no circumstances should the abdomen be touched.

If a hospital cage is not available, the same effect can be achieved by using a show cage and placing it with the open front close to a source of heat. A thermometer must be placed inside the cage and a careful watch kept upon it to ensure that the interior does not become too hot.

Like the remarks made on fighting between cocks and hens, the beginner must not take this subject too much to heart. It is the exception rather than the given rule, and provided that the hens are given sufficient calcium and the bird room is kept to 50 degrees as advised, there should be no such occurrence. Since such problems do occur from time to time, however, they must of course be mentioned.

Many beginners worry about egg binding, usually because they have never seen a hen in this condition, and wonder whether they will recognise it if it does occur. Unless the beginner is completely lacking in common sense, the signs will be all too apparent. The hen will be either in the nest box, refusing to leave when the bottom is tapped, or will be found on the floor of the cage with her feathers fluffed out and will be very obviously in some distress. It is possible that when the bird is taken in the hand the end of the egg may be seen at the entrance to the oviduct. When a hen is seen in this condition, the treatment described above should be carried out immediately. There can be no 'wait and see', and it cannot be stressed sufficiently strongly that immediate action must be taken.

HATCHING

The first egg will hatch after 18 days, and at this point a very controversial issue must be raised. Some fanciers believe that the chicks should be helped from the shell if they are in difficulty, while others believe that under no circumstances should this operation be carried out.

In order to understand the two arguments, one should be made aware of the methods used by the chick in its attempts to escape from its shell. While it is in the egg, the chick develops a small spike on the end of its beak, the so called egg tooth. With this 'tooth', it gradually breaks a circle in the shell causing it to break into halves, and allowing its occupant to escape. During the time that the chick is developing, it is fed from the substance of the egg, the white, by what in human terms would be the umbilical cord. Through this cord, the white of the egg is absorbed into the body of the chick, and not until the chick is fully prepared in terms of adequate growth to face the outside world, is the cord broken, whereupon the chick emerges from the egg.

Figure 7.7 Infertile Eggs should be left in the Nest to help prevent crushing of the Chicks through the weight of the Hen

The amount of food taken from inside the egg by the chick is generally considered to sustain the small creature for two days, irrespective of whether it is fed by the parents or not. Not until that amount of food has passed from the egg into the body of the chick will the cord be broken, and if it is broken before the correct time, then the chick will certainly die.

This being so, any attempt by the fancier to assist a chick by breaking the shell must be undertaken with extreme caution, and, what is more, at exactly the right time.

At about sixteen days, the chick should be heard tapping inside the egg; on the seventeenth day a brown line and a hole will appear, possibly accompanied by minute hair like crack. At the same time, the chick will be clearly heard cheeping inside the egg. On the eighteenth day, the chick should have completed the circumference of the egg and should emerge. Not until the end of the eighteenth day should any attempt be made to help the chick to emerge, and many fanciers would argue that it should not be done in any event.

If the decision is made to help the chick, however, this must be done with extreme caution, using a feather quill.

First, make a small puncture in the end of the egg at its broad end where the head will lie. Then, taking great care, gradually chip away the end of the shell, allowing the chick to free itself. At that stage, and when a large enough hole has been made the chick should be left to its own devices. If an attempt is made to extricate the chick fully, then it will almost certainly cause bleeding.

The fanciers who argue against this operation are of the opinion that a chick which is not strong enough to be able to extricate itself from the shell is suffering from some inherited weakening trait, or is in itself too weak and probably not of the desired quality. There may be quite a lot of truth in that argument, but there are other reasons why a perfectly healthy and normally developed chick is unable to escape from its shell.

This concerns the humidity of the nest box. The theory is that if the interior of the bird room is too dry, the membrane surrounding the chick while it is inside the egg is dried up and becomes too tough for the bird to break through, and also holds the chick, preventing it from being able to turn around inside the shell and to complete its task of circling the egg. There are two ways of overcoming this problem, though neither is very satisfactory in my view.

The first is that water trays should be placed on top of the heaters, evaporating the water and dampening the atmosphere in the bird room. The second method is to soak the eggs in warm water at a temperature of about 70 degrees Fahrenheit for (20C) for about twenty minutes on the sixteenth day. Neither of these methods can be said to be foolproof, but they will certainly help to eliminate the problem. Some fanciers have the habit of holding the eggs in the mouth for a few minutes at the sixteenth day and swear by this method. Whether there is any real merit in that, however, is a matter for debate and I would not care to give an opinion either way.

Another cause of dead in shell is, as stated above, the possibility of an inherent defect in the chicks passed down to them from the parents. If one has two nests of chicks in one season, all or most of which are dead in shell, then this is a possible cause and the pair should not be used for breeding again. Conversely, it may be that the weather has been very arid and has dried out the atmosphere to such an extent that most of the eggs in the entire bird room contain dead in shell.

If such a season is encountered, then all or most of the breeders in the same area will probably be experiencing similar troubles, in which case the cause may safely be put down to the weather, and some means of overcoming the problem must be found. If the problem is confined to one's own bird room, however, and everyone else appears to be having a normal breeding season, then there must obviously be some other cause.

Lack of iodine is said to be one such cause, but if the feeding programme has been carried out as suggested, there should be no trouble in that respect. If the individual fancier wishes to guard against this, however, blocks known as iodine nibbles are available from pet shops and will certainly solve the problems of lack of iodine even if they do not solve the problem of dead in shell.

FOSTERING

When the chicks have hatched, then fostering may become necessary, and if the chicks are to be removed then this should be done at a time when the fancier is able to spend some time in the bird room observing the stock. The cock in particular may not take kindly to a strange chick, and may attack and kill it. If the cock begins to show signs of this form of behaviour, then the chick should be removed immediately and put under another pair.

The young chicks will be moved on the first day on which they hatch, and if they have been marked as described, there will be no problem in identifying them later, because at five to seven days they will be ringed with their own individual ring number duly recorded, following which there will be no problems in ascertaining which chick came from which pair.

When chicks are being fostered by another pair, it is important that they should be placed in nests with chicks of approximately the same

103

age. If a chick is placed in a nest box where the eggs have not yet begun to hatch, then the hen will almost certainly reject the new chick.

It should also be pointed out that apart from special circumstances such as, for example, the death of the hen, chicks should not be fostered after the age of about twelve days. After that time, they will almost certainly be rejected by the cock.

NIGHT LIGHTS

At the start of the breeding season, most breeders bring night lights into operation — small 20 watt blue lights. The use of this very much reduced form of lighting will allow the hen to leave the nest box during the night for feeding purposes, should she so wish, and what is perhaps more important, will allow her to find her way back to the nest box and the chicks within. The number of such lights will depend, of course, on the size of the bird room, but sufficient should be used to allow the hen to be able to see, without the bird room being too brightly lit during the night.

FOOD FOR THE CHICKS

The most important food, so far as the feeding of young Budgerigars is concerned, is the soft food. The constitution of this has already been discussed, and starting from the sixteenth day after the first egg has been laid, this type of food should be offered three times daily. It should be given once in the early morning, at around noon, and again at night about half an hour before the lights are due to begin to dim. The birds will eat the fresh soft food every time it is introduced to the cage, and the purpose of giving it early in the morning just after dawn is to ensure that the parents feed the young birds as quickly as possible after their nightly fast.

There is an even more important reason for giving soft food just before dusk. The reader will no doubt recall the chapter on feeding and the remarks made concerning the provision of grit, and, more importantly the description of the crop. The young chicks will be fed at dusk with sufficient food to fill their crops, and this will sustain them throughout the night. Introducing fresh soft food at dusk will help to ensure that this process is carried out by the parents, and is also the main reason for the use of a dimmer switch.

If the lights are suddenly switched off leaving the birds plunged into total darkness, there is nothing to suggest that the young chicks have recently been fed; in fact, it may be as much as two hours since feeding took place. Such a circumstance is rather dangerous in view of the frequency at which young birds must be fed, and I stress the word *must*. Only if the birds believe that dusk is falling will it be certain that the chicks will be fed at any given time, and all possible precautions must be taken to ensure that this is the case.

Also at this time, when the parent birds have fed their young, a check should be made on every nest box and every chick to make sure that the crop is full. This can easily be seen because the skin at the base of the neck beneath which the crop lies is translucent and the food inside is visible. If the crop is empty, or only partially full, steps must be taken to fill it.

This is by no means so difficult as it sounds and may be achieved quite easily with the aid of a small syringe filled with a sloppy mixture of bread and milk.

Take the bird in the left hand, assuming the breeder is right handed, and with the end of the syringe, minus the needle, gently stroke the beak. The bird will gape for food, and the end of the syringe can be inserted and a small amount of food expelled. Take care not to put too much food into the beak at one time, because, especially in very young chicks, this can cause blockage of the air passages and subsequent suffocation. When the breeder is satisfied that the crop is sufficiently full, the chick may be returned to the nest.

Some breeders give a feed of soft food at around tea time, especially in the summer months when the weather is hot. Hard boiled egg will turn sour very rapidly indeed in hot weather, and if the temperature in the bird room does become excessive, this may well happen. In such circumstances it is wise to change the soft food as frequently as is practicable thus ensuring that no stale food is taken in by either the parents or through them, by the young birds. This point is very important because the ingestion of stale food is a major cause of diseases affecting the digestive tract, even mild forms of which would quickly kill a young bird.

Fresh soaked groats, which have been soaked for twenty-four hours and well strained should be offered daily, as also should soaked seed which has been allowed to sprout in the manner previously described in the chapter on feeding. Some fanciers mix greenfood in with the soft food in small quantities, and I see nothing wrong with that practice. At this point, however, it is perhaps best to feed only the lightest types of greenfood, leaving out the brassica type of vegetable leaf because of its tendency to scour. This tendency would become even more pronounced in the case of young chicks, and it might fairly be argued that this is a bad practice.

Many fanciers cut out the feed of soft food at noon, and substitute a feed of wholemeal bread and milk as previously described. Again, because of the vitamin content of the wholemeal, specially the salts, I see nothing wrong with this practice. It must be stressed, however, that such food must be removed from the breeding cages before the milk turns sour — for obvious reasons.

There is no necessity to make up a fresh batch of soft food for each feed. If the food is made up in the morning and is kept in a cool place then it will be perfectly in order to supply this to the birds for the remainder of the day. A fresh batch must be made up each day, however. The words, 'a cool place', do not refer to the refrigerator; bringing food out of a refrigerator and feeding the birds with it will produce gastric chills and will be very harmful to the stock.

Many breeders have no choice but to leave the birds sufficient food for the day, or at least from morning to around five in the evening. There is nothing at all wrong in this method, but if, because of personal circumstances the fancier must do this, then he should make certain that each cage has a sufficient supply of all the types of food offered. Care will have to be taken here. As the chicks grow, which as we have seen is a very rapid process, they will need relatively larger amounts of food each day, and whereas a nest of four–day old chicks may require perhaps only one tablespoon of soft food each day, when they are perhaps eight days old, this amount may well need to be at least doubled.

There is no stipulated amount of food. Each pair of birds will take only the amounts they need, and the golden rule is to supply more than one believes is necessary. If, for example, the hen decides that she needs soft food and comes out of the nest box only to find that there is no food available of the type she needs, then she may well desert the nest.

RINGING THE CHICKS

When the chicks are no more than five days old, their closed rings must be fitted. This operation worries many newcomers who have not carried it out previously, but it is a very simple operation, and with practice can be accomplished very quickly indeed.

It should be pointed out that with some chicks, the precise time of ringing may be a little flexible to say the least. Some chicks have larger than average feet while others have smaller. In the case of a chick with larger than average feet, ringing at four days may be better. It should also be pointed out that when the chicks are seven days old, their feet will have grown to such an extent that it may be impossible to ring them.

The method of ringing is really very simple. Take the chick in the left hand, and with the right, push the ring over the three longer toes, up the ball of the foot and as high as it will comfortably go up the hock. At this

106

stage, the much shorter back toe will be held against the leg, with the point at which the toe joins the foot forming a U shape. With the end of a burned match stick, insert the point beneath the U, and gently ease the toe back through the ring, holding the bird in the palm of the left hand, and the three long toes between thumb and forefinger. There is only one point to watch, and that is not to put the match stick under the toe and flick it out. This may result in the claw being ripped off, a highly undesirable state of affairs. Simply work the pointed end of the match stick gently through, and all will be well.

It may seem difficult for some fanciers to believe, but I have come across cases where the rings have been taken up the leg, over the 'knee' joint and on to the thigh. This, of course, becomes far too tight when the thigh begins to broaden out and can cause gangrene by constricting the blood vessels. Because of that, it must be made perfectly clear that rings should be placed on the **lower leg**, between the knee and the 'ankle'.

One other point which must be very carefully noted is that, after the chicks have been ringed, a careful check should be made on each one for the next forty-eight hours. It is by no means unknown for rings to slip back over the foot while the chicks are in the nest box, and the fancier should make sure that the rings have remained on the chicks when he examines the nest boxes.

Some fanciers also place a split celluloid ring on the other leg of the chicks for identification purposes, but it is not necessary to do this at the same time as closed ringing is carried out. The split type of ring can be put on the bird at any age and is a very simple operation indeed. The ring is simply slipped over a specially made tool and pushed up a channelled end until it is sufficiently wide to go over the lower leg of the bird. The ring and leg are held together between thumb and forefinger and the tool is gently withdrawn, upon which the ring closes around the leg. Although this is not essential, it is a very good method of instant identification if all the chicks from one nest are ringed with the same coloured ring. Positive identification can be achieved, of course, by looking at the number on the closed ring and reference to one's records. As each bird is closed rung, the number of the ring is entered immediately on its record card.

FEATHERING

At about seven days, the chicks will begin to grow their feathers. This first appears as a fine grey down on the back and head, and gradually becomes thicker until about the age of fifteen days, when the bird should be almost completely covered. One week later, when the chick is three weeks old, the feathers will look like feathers, and the breeder will know

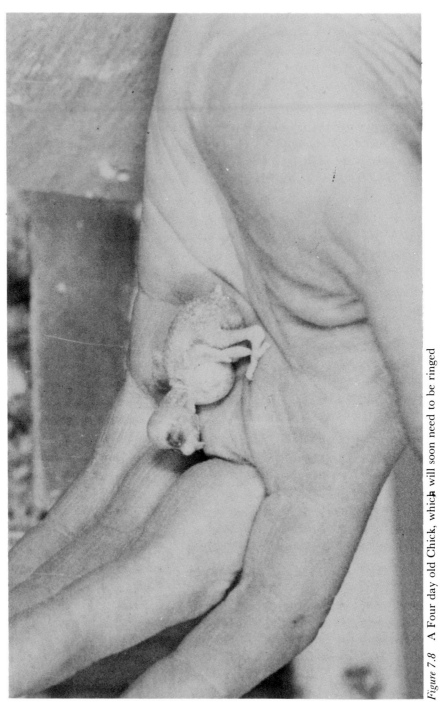

Figure 7.8 A Four day old Chick, which will soon need to be ringed

exactly what colour the bird will be. At this stage, the beginner may have some difficulty in ascertaining whether the bird is a normal or an opaline, because all young chicks retain the bars around the head and neck. A tip for beginners is that on the wing of an opaline, at the point at which the primary flights emerge from the secondaries about half way up the wing, a clear patch can be seen on the edge of each wing. A young barhead which has this patch is an opaline. The term 'barhead' is frequently used by breeders to describe Budgerigars from this stage until after their first moult, when the bars will, or, especially in the case of opalines, should disappear.

Crop Gases

During the time between the hatching of the chicks and their being feathered, there is one extremely important point of which very careful note should be made. When the very young chicks are being examined, a very careful observation should be made on the state of the crop. Obviously one must look to make sure that there is a sufficient amount of food in the crop, but also at this time, gases are frequently produced in the crop, which distend it to a positively alarming degree. Fortunately, the distention of the crop by gases rather than by food can clearly be seen because of the translucent nature of the skin as described earlier. If a chick is found in such a state, there is a very easy method of dealing with the problem.

Take the chick into the palm of the hand, and with the forefinger of the other hand, very gently stroke the crop from the bottom towards the beak. Only a light pressure is required and, after a few moments, the chick will give a distinct 'burp', and some of the gas will be expelled. Continue the treatment until the crop resumes its normal size. This is precisely the same operation as that used with babies when stroking their backs to get their wind up. The condition if allowed to continue will certainly cause distress to the young bird, and may, in very extreme cases, cause even worse problems.

UNDERSHOT BEAK

Another possible source of trouble, especially in smaller chicks, are the circumstances which lead to a condition known as **undershot beak**. In this condition, the upper mandible ceases to grow, while the lower continues to grow to its normal length. This, when the beak is fully developed, results in a bird, the beak of which has the lower mandible overlapping the upper instead of the other way round. Such a bird is useless for showing or for breeding, since it will be unable to feed its chicks correctly.

109

This is caused by the chick not swallowing all of its food, especially soft food. Particles lodge under the upper mandible and gradually build up, setting to a hard consistency, and retarding the growth of the beak. Again, treatment is quite simple, and consists merely of checking the underside of the upper mandible when the chicks are being examined in the normal routine manner.

All that needs to be done is to take a pointed matchstick, and to remove the uneaten food, which will immediately solve the problem.

FEATHER PLUCKING

When the young chicks begin the grow their feathers, the possibility of feather plucking may arise. This is a very frustrating habit so far as the breeder is concerned, and is an extremely difficult problem to solve. The offender may be either the cock or the hen, and many theories have been put forward from time to time as to the cause.

Some believe that the cause is hereditary, and this is one possibility. Whether it is hereditary in the Budgerigar alone, however, is a completely different matter, since Budgerigars are by no means the only species to indulge in this practice. Canary fanciers have the same problem when there are young chicks in the nest, and in general, they believe that the hens will pluck the chicks to use the feathers for lining the nest. Since Budgerigars do not build a nest, but still indulge in feather plucking, that idea may be erroneous. Likewise, foreign species, the smaller species especially, are notorious for this, and will feather pluck their mates or companions at any time of the year, whether breeding or not.

This must surely bring one to the conclusion that feather plucking is certainly not confined to Budgerigars, nor to one particular pair, but is an inherent factor in most birds. The question, therefore, of whether this trait can be bred out of a stud is, in my opinion, very debatable, although there can be little doubt that some birds are more prone to feather plucking than others.

There is no real solution to this problem, except perhaps to refrain from breeding with such birds in the following season if the problem becomes too bad. If it occurs in a nest, it may help to place a clean nest box inside the cage and transfer the chicks to that, leaving the hen to settle down for the second round, and the cock to feed the chicks. Whether he will do so is another matter. If this method is adopted, then a very close watch will have to be kept on the cage for the next two days to make sure that the cock is in fact feeding. Failing that, the chicks could be transferred to another nest, but this is dangerous at this stage, because the cock of the foster pair will almost certainly view the new chick as a rival for the affections of his mate and will probably act accordingly.

SITTING TOO TIGHTLY

Yet another problem may arise when the chicks are very small. Sometimes, the breeder will examine the nest box, and will find a chick or chicks with legs spread out at right angles to the body. This condition is caused by the hen sitting too tightly and placing her full weight on the chicks. There is nothing which can be done to put the matter right, and in such a case the chick should be painlessly destroyed immediately. Do not be tempted to keep the chick in the hope that the condition will right itself, it will not, and the only humane solution is to put the chick down.

As a precaution against this occurrence, most fanciers leave any unhatched eggs in the nest. If the eggs are left, they will make space under the hen for the small chicks. While this may not be a one hundred per cent certain method of ensuring that the situation will not arise, it is certainly a good defence against it happening.

THE SECOND ROUND

We now come to the most critical time of all, the time at which the pair are ready to go to nest for their second round, but while the chicks from the first round are still in the nest box. This situation is dangerous for two main reasons.

The first, and most obvious, is that the first round chicks may break the second round eggs, and the second is that the hen may deliberately try to drive the chicks out of the nest box by pecking their heads, perhaps causing permanent damage. Another possibility is that the cock will see the chicks as potential rivals and will attack them for that reason. Alternatively, he may try to mate with them, and on finding this not acceptable to the chicks, will then turn on them out of sheer frustration.

All of this will begin when the first round chicks are five weeks old, and at this stage, they cannot be taken away from their parents, but have to be weaned to hard seed in the same manner as a baby is weaned on to solid food.

WEANING THE CHICKS

Usually, if all is well, the chicks will begin to leave the nest box at five weeks. When they have begun to do so, they will be fed in the cage by the cock, while the hen continues to lay her second round. Most birds will be ready to be taken away from the stock cage ten days after leaving the nest box, and many fanciers believe that they should not remain in the breeding cage for any longer than this.

My view, and I am sure that of most experienced breeders, however, is that young Budgerigars are very much individual personalities. Just as some develop physically more rapidly than others, so some develop self sufficiency more quickly than others. The ones which are slow to learn may take twelve days or even longer to learn to crack hard seed, and caution is advised.

While the chicks are out of the nest box but still in the parents' cage, the normal adult diet of soaked seed and soaked groats will be placed in the cage daily. The young birds will almost certainly begin to eat the softer seed first, and not until they have been outside the nest box for perhaps nine days will they begin to crack the hard seed. Only when they are seen to do so with ease and obvious enjoyment should they be removed from the parents' cage; certainly not before twelve days if there is any doubt. It would be true to state that by far the majority of young birds are quite ready to leave the breeding cage after ten days, however, and although this is an anxious time for the beginner, if careful observation has been made there should be little trouble.

There is one extremely important point which should be noted here. If, after keeping a close watch on the young birds, the decision has finally been made to remove them, the birds should not be put back into their parents' cage under any circumstances. If they are, the cock will certainly attack them. The birds will sit on the perches or the floor of the cage calling pathetically for food, but their cries must be ignored and they must now be left to their own devices.

It is at this point that the cages with removable slides between come into play. When the young birds have been removed from the breeding cage, they should be placed in a similar cage, preferably placed so that they are unable to see the parents. Wide shallow dishes of soaked seed and groats should be placed in the cage, along with a similar dish of hard seed. After two days, the slide between the weaning cage and the next cage can be removed, allowing the birds more room, once they have become accustomed to the positioning of their food on the cage floor.

Having had their chicks removed the parents will now carry on with their second round in exactly the same manner as before.

When the second round eggs are due to be laid, and if the first round chicks have left the nest box before the hen has begun to lay, the breeder must not forget to check each nest box every day for purposes of keeping his records up to date. There is also the possibility, of course, that a hen may become egg bound during the laying of the second round eggs,

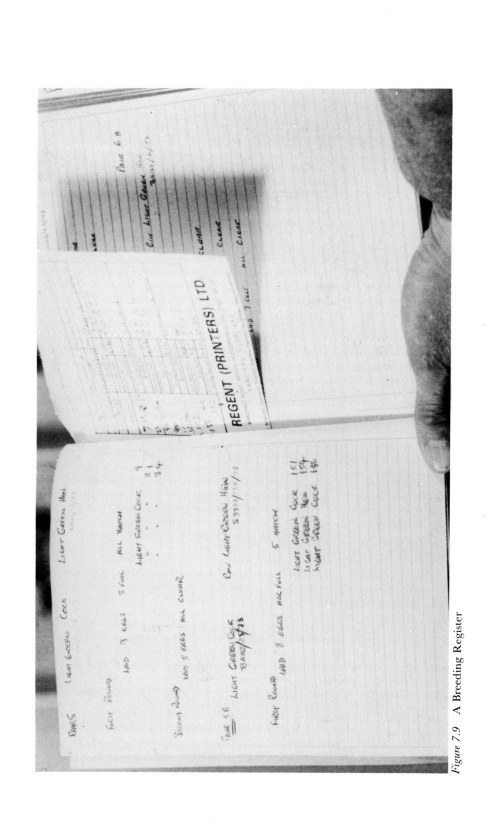

Figure 7.9 A Breeding Register

although this is less probable than with the first round. This may appear to be stating the obvious, but it is very easy to continue to pay attention to the chicks and not to pay sufficient attention to the parents.

THE BREEDING REGISTER

As soon as the first round chicks are removed from the breeding cage, a breeding register should be started. The details on the breeding cards are transferred to the register, and at this point, the breeder will know how many eggs were laid in the first round; how many were fertile or infertile; how many of the chicks survived; and the reasons for the death of any which did not survive. The ring numbers and colour of the parents should be entered; the colours of the chicks produced, including any which were not reared, together with their celluloid rings if these have been used. Space should be left for the sex of the chicks when this becomes known after the first moult and the ceres begin to take on their brown or blue colouring. Breeding problems should also be noted, so that the breeder will know what to expect in the following breeding season if he wishes to use that particular bird again.

There should also be a record of the good and bad points of parents and chicks; careful analysis of these when the time comes to pair them up with other birds will give much useful knowledge. Such matters as for example feather plucking can also be pinpointed. If there have been problems in a particular cage and the breeder is not certain about which of the pair was the offender, he notes the fact. If he then pairs the birds up with different mates in the following season and the same thing happens in one cage, then he can be reasonably sure of which bird is responsible.

The importance of keeping records cannot be too strongly stressed. It is quite easy to remember which bird came from which pair when the chicks are young, have had individual attention daily, and are easily recognisable as individuals. Over the weeks, memory will certainly fade and therefore the only certain way of making sure that no point is forgotten, is to keep accurate daily records, recording each fact or incident on the day it takes place.

PROBLEMS IN THE BREEDING SEASON

Dirty Feet

During their period in the nest boxes, the chicks will move around in the dried excreta in the concave. As a result of this, their toes will become gradually coated, and the result will be that a small ball will collect on each toe. On no account should this ball be pulled off, because if this is

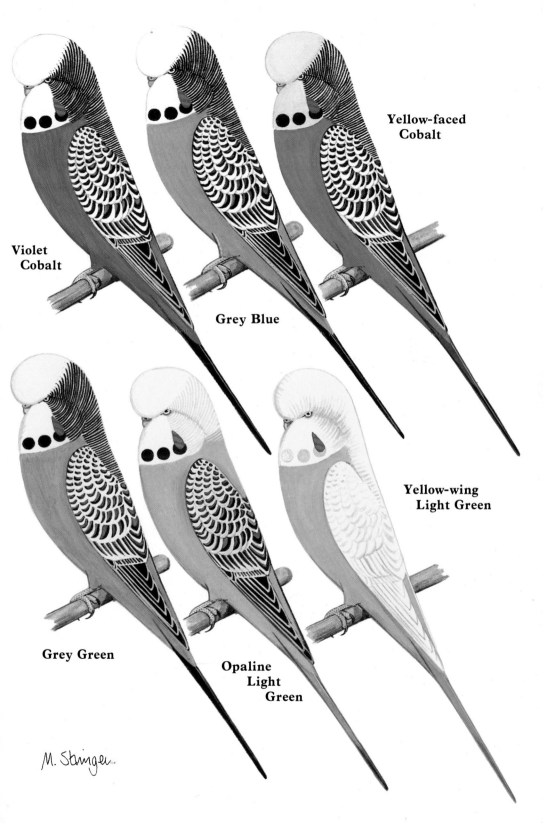

Violet
Cobalt

Grey Blue

Yellow-faced
Cobalt

Grey Green

Opaline
Light
Green

Yellow-wing
Light Green

M. Stringer.

Plate 2 — Various Budgerigars.

attempted, there is a danger that the claw will be pulled off with it. The correct method of removal is to soak the foot in warm water for a few moments until the ball becomes softened and then to remove it. This is a perfectly normal occurrence and is not a sign of anything untoward.

Starvation of the Parents

A far more serious problem is that of the starvation of the parents. This is more likely to happen to the hen, but the cock may also suffer the same fate. The reason is that the hen will take the crop milk from the cock continually to feed the chicks, and concentrates so much on them that she neglects to feed herself.

There are, of course, several combinations of this problem. The hen may die while incubating, not for the reasons stated, but simply because she is sitting too tight and will not leave her clutch even to feed herself. Under these circumstances all that can be done is to mark the eggs as previously described and transfer them to another pair.

If the hen should die while there are chicks in the nest not yet feathered, then similar action must be taken. The cock may well continue to feed the chicks, but it is unlikely that he will sit on them to keep them warm, in which case they will become chilled and will die.

If the chicks have their feathers, however, and fostering out is impracticable because of the differing ages of the chicks in another nest or some similar reason, the cock may be left with the chicks and because they are feathered, they will in all probability be successfully reared, assuming of course that the cock continues to carry out his duties.

If the cock dies, and the chicks cannot be transferred, then the hen may be left to rear the brood alone, but a careful watch must be kept on her to see that she is feeding herself. It may well be that the hen is more valuable than the chicks and, if that is so, and she appears not to be feeding herself correctly, then the decision will have to be made on whether the chicks should be transferred with the risk of their being attacked by the foster cock, in order to save the hen, or whether the hen should be allowed to continue in the hope that she will manage to rear them.

It should be pointed out here, that there are distinct signs of one or both parents neglecting themselves for the sake of their young. Most birds, cocks and hens alike begin to lose weight during the breeding season. Bringing up a nest of four chicks is a very great drain on their energies and physical resources. Under such circumstances some physical signs of the strain under which the parents are placed are inevitable. If, however, the birds appear to be losing too much weight, particularly if the breast bone begins to protrude unnaturally, then something is amiss and immediate action must be taken.

115

If the hen is the problem, then there is little which can be done except hope for the best, unless, of course the chicks can be fostered. In the case of the cock underfeeding himself, he may be taken out of the breeding cage for an hour or so each morning, preferably just after the chicks have been fed and put in a nearby stock cage. After he has fed himself, he can then be returned.

Desertion of the Nest

Sometimes, the parents will desert the chicks for no apparent reason. There are two main reasons for hens deserting the nest; one is too much interference by the fancier, and the other is inadequate feeding.

The nests must be examined morning and night for reasons we have already discussed, but at such times, there should be only the minimum interference by the fancier. Do only what is necessary and under no circumstances keep the hen away from the nest any longer than is essential. Continually forcing the hen off the nest and into the breeding cage will eventually lead to her losing confidence in the privacy of the nest, and the inevitable result of that will be desertion.

Cleaning of the cages must be kept to an absolute minimum for the same reasons, and this is why a thorough cleaning of the cage before breeding operations actually begin is absolutely essential.

All possible sources of extraneous noise must be found and eliminated. These, while they may not be a problem during the day, will certainly cause frights during the night and must be avoided. Visitors should either be kept to a minimum, or banned entirely from the bird room during the breeding season. Many experienced fanciers adopt the latter method for the same reasons as given above.

The general rules concerning noise in the bird room do not apply in the breeding season. The breeder should go about feeding and attending to his stock in as quiet a manner as possible, making no more noise than is absolutely necessary.

Ending the Breeding Season

Most breeders consider, in my view quite correctly, that two full nests of chicks are quite enough for one pair to rear during any one breeding season. If the hen has had to bring up two or more chicks in both nests, then she should be prevented from further breeding activity.

If, however, she has had her eggs transferred for any reason — perhaps the death of the cock during the incubation period — or has had her chicks transferred at an early age, then this may be discounted and a third round may be taken. These are generalisations, and the breeder should pay close attention to the general health of the hen before allowing her to continue.

Remember that the hen will have spent something like four months in the nest box by the time the third round chicks are hatched, which is in itself debilitating, and if there is any doubt at all about the fitness of the hen to undertake the extra work, then operations should cease immediately.

It may be that the hen will begin to lay before the second round chicks are ready to leave the nest, and if this is the case, allow her to finish laying her clutch; get the second round chicks away from the breeding cage, and then remove the nest box. Split the pair up, but do not replace them in the flights. Put them into the small stock flights, and for the first two weeks after breeding, continue to give all of the diet which has been offered during the breeding season. This will help to replace the lost weight, and the placing of the birds in the small cage type flights will allow them that much needed rest which they have surely earned.

Not until the breeder believes that the birds are fully recovered from their breeding activities should they be replaced in the larger flights.

Remembering the end of the chapter on general management of the stud, similar remarks apply to the breeding season. It should be obvious that one would not open a nest box with very small chicks in it and fill it with the fumes of a red mite spray, and then close the lid. Equally if a cage or nest box becomes more than acceptably dirty then some attempt must be made to clean it, and once again, common sense must play a part.

All breeders experience problems which are peculiar to them in their own personal circumstances, and in such cases, it is a matter of using initiative and common sense to find a solution. In general, it could be fairly said that if there are problems in the breeding room, they are probably the fault of the breeder and not the stock.

One final point concerns the remarks made in the chapter on feeding. The breeder is advised that if he has a good system of feeding which is acceptable to the stock and is maintaining them in good general health then this should not be changed. This also applies to the breeding season. If all is going well, then carry on with whatever method is being used. There is a saying, 'never change a winning combination', and nothing could be closer to the truth than when that is applied to Budgerigar breeding. Again, by all means experiment, that is the way to progress, but until the results of such experiments have been assessed and proved to be better than the methods already in use, follow the same routines. Remember that while experimentation, if carried out in a proper manner, can be a very good idea in any stud, one should not carry out such experiments with one's best birds. So far as they are concerned, following the methods which you know very well will bring good results.

We have mentioned a large number of problems which may arise during the breeding season, but the beginner in particular should be made aware that these problems are very much the exception. If the birds are well fed, well housed, and left alone as much as possible in quiet, clean and relatively warm surroundings then all should be well.

Figure 7.10   A good Show Specimen *Courtesy:* **Cage and Aviary Birds**

CHAPTER 8

THE SHOW SEASON

SHOW PREPARATION

The next stage in the breeding and rearing of Exhibition Budgerigars is extremely important for the would-be exhibitor. This period will have a most profound effect upon the performance of the birds at shows, and may well make the difference between a good bird being a winner or an 'also ran'. The emphasis during the next few weeks must be on the training of the young birds, and the instilling of an inherent showmanship. While it is true that showmanship can, and frequently is, bred into a bird, there are few which cannot be trained to stand correctly and fearlessly for the judge, provided that the breeder goes the correct way about the matter.

When the young birds are separated from their parents, they are placed in the cage flights as previously described. Since there will be several cages in a single long unit, this means logically that there will be several doors. Old show cages, the doors of which have been removed, or specially built cages of similar dimensions to those of a show cage, should be hung on perhaps three of the doors and left permanently in that position.

The young birds will begin to investigate the interiors of the cages very quickly, and, equally quickly, will begin to spend some of their time sitting in them. As with nest boxes, the fancier should, of course make sure that the cages are very firmly fixed to the front of the cage and cannot be knocked off.

TO HANDLE, OR NOT?

At this stage, a somewhat controversial question is raised. Some breeders believe that it is better to handle one's birds, on the premise

119

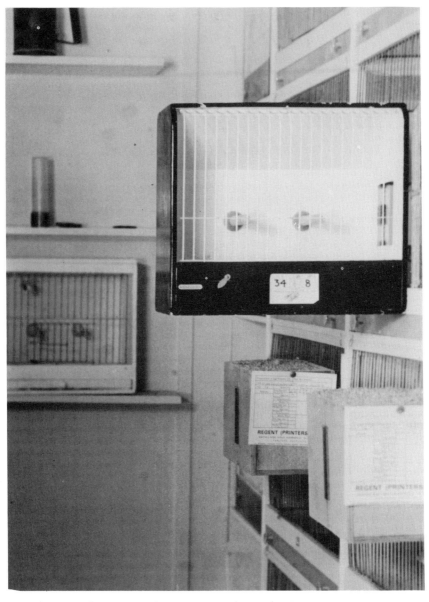

Figure 8.1   A Show Cage hanging on a Stock Cage, a method which allows the young birds to become quickly accustomed to it

that when they are being prepared for a show then they may well have to be handled in any event for purposes of trimming the mask and spots or perhaps cutting the nails. Others do not believe in handling the birds more than is necessary, in the belief that this frightens them and will cause them to be afraid in the close proximity to people at a show.

The question is difficult to answer, because clearly both theories have merit. Neither is there any room for compromise, one must decide either to handle or not according to one's personal assessment of the situation.

There is one point heavily in favour of the first theory, however, which must be at least drawn to the attention of the reader. When the young birds are placed in what we will now term the 'training flights', they are quite familiar with being handled in the normal course of inspection of the breeding cages. Indeed, at this stage, most of the birds can be finger trained should the fancier wish, but this practice is not advisable in show stock. Clearly, the stock will have to be handled at some stage, and in my view, the more familiar they are with this situation the better. A bird which is not familiar with being handled is probably far more prone to being frightened by it than one which is familiar with the situation.

If the decision is made to handle birds then, preferably each day, each one should be carefully removed from the cage, and simply be picked up and held in the hand for a few moments. It should be pointed out here that there are correct and incorrect methods of handling Budgerigars. The correct method is to hold the bird in the palm of the hand with the thumb and forefinger around the neck, firmly, but not too tightly for very obvious reasons! The bird should then be turned on its back, the wings being held close to the sides with the ball of the thumb on one side and the little finger on the other. In such a position, the bird will in all probability cease to struggle, especially so because Budgerigars do not like to be turned on their backs.

Hold the bird like this for a few moments, gently stroking the mask and head, following which procedure, place it back in the show cage, when it will fly back into the training flight leaving the cage for the next bird.

THE TRAINING UNIT

If, as described in the chapter on housing, a training unit has been built, the birds should be placed in this after about two weeks in the training flights.

Seed and water should be provided in the same manner as they are normally in a show cage, but in the first instance, the birds should not be left for very long periods — an hour is quite enough. At first, the birds will take some time to settle down, but if they are familiarised with the

Figure 8.2   The correct way of holding a Bird

show cage, as described, they will soon adapt. The birds will have a completely unfamiliar view of the bird room, and will be closely confined for the first time. Obviously under such unfamiliar circumstances they must be allowed some time to settle.

At first they may climb on the bars of the cage, or spend most of the time on the cage floors, but, again, if they have been trained in the manner first described, such behaviour will not continue for very long. The time which the young birds spend in the show cages is then gradually increased until they are quite happy to spend a full day in the training unit.

Training Problems

There are three main problems concerning the training of the young birds, and they are those most commonly met with at shows.

The first, and most common of all, is the bird which refuses to stand on its perch, and spends all of its time on the floor of the cage, possibly with its head beneath the drinker. These problems, in my opinion, are not caused by any inherent fear of the perches, but are obvious signs of fear of the close proximity of people. Such birds are probably very unfamiliar with being peered at by total strangers at close quarters, and, quite naturally they react by hiding in a corner or under the drinker.

The most probable cause of this type of behaviour is that the breeder has not spent sufficient time in the bird room during the training period, or, if he has, then he has spent that time at the other end of the bird room away from the training unit or cages.

Sometimes, however, this problem arises, when no matter how much time the breeder spends close by the cages, the young bird will continue with this behaviour. In that case, it is quite a simple matter to remove the bird from a training cage into a show cage, and then to turn this upside down. Because of the sloping roof, the bird will continually slide toward the front where it will press on the bars; it will be cramped and most uncomfortable. The only way in which it can be comfortable under those conditions is to go up to the perches — which it will do quite quickly. This simple solution will usually solve that particular problem.

The second problem is that of birds which persistently cling to the bars of the cage, usually biting them and chipping off the paint, and refusing absolutely to stand on the perches. Again, there is quite a simple remedy for this type of behaviour.

A piece of glass, or preferably perspex, should be cut to the required size, and fixed inside the cage front close to the bars. This will certainly solve the immediate problem, but with a bird exhibiting this type of behaviour, the perspex should be left in position for a few days until the bird grasps the idea that it cannot hold the bars of the cage front.

The third problem is much more serious. Even if a bird is accustomed to the confines of a show cage, it may well be that it will refuse to stand at the correct angle. One may or may not be able to solve this particular problem, depending upon the adaptability of the bird, which is of course an unknown quantity.

In a case of this nature, the perspex should be placed in the cage, and on the outside, a piece of cardboard is fastened which should reach the point where the neck of the bird should be. We have already referred to the innate inquisitiveness of Budgerigars, and the bird will undoubtedly be intrigued to know what is going on outside the show cage. In all probability it will stretch up to be able to peer over the top of the cardboard, and this will teach it the correct stance.

Sometimes the problem can be solved by the use of this method in a matter of two or three days, but occasionally a bird may be in the show cage for perhaps two weeks, and immediately the card is removed will return to its old habits. Sometimes, unfortunately, no amount of such training will combat the problem, and in such cases the bird concerned must be discarded for show purposes — perhaps even for breeding purposes as well unless it is a very high quality bird in other respects.

A Break in Training

Some fanciers do not believe in continuing show training during the moult. This, so far as the young birds are concerned, will start at the age of ten weeks. At this point, the birds are in the process of exchanging their nest feathers for adult plumage, and consequently are growing new feathers.

The reader must be told that the feathers of a Budgerigar are formed almost completely from protein or protein derivatives, and it follows, therefore, that proteins which are normally used for the body building process are being diluted because of some of the protein is being used for the formation of the new feathers. More will be said on this subject later, but this situation can affect the training programme, and that aspect of the problem is properly discussed at this point.

Because the proteins in the diet are being used in feather formation, it follows that they are not being used in the normal manner by the body processes. As a consequence, the birds, while not being in a generally unhealthy state, are certainly not up to their usual level of stamina. Taking them from the stock cages each day and forcing them to spend hours in a show cage while in such a delicate condition is not advisable. Most experienced fanciers would probably agree with this for the period of the moult, which, as a general guide, will take about eight weeks depending on the bird. Not until the young bird has finished moulting

124

should full show training be re-started, but during the time that the birds are replaced in the training flights for the first moult, the training cages can be replaced on the cage fronts.

The breeder should not be afraid that after this break training will need to be started all over again. The birds will have had five weeks of training before stopping for the moult, and it is perfectly true that what they learn early in life they will never forget. After the moult has ended, however, training can be started again for perhaps two or three weeks to make sure that the birds have remembered their early training.

It should be noted that the moult of a young bird is something of a mystery in terms of time. Sometimes, they will have cast their feathers and will have grown their new ones within six weeks. Other birds, however, may shed only a few feathers at a time and may take up to ten weeks or even longer to fully moult out. Most breeders would agree that the quicker the moult the better. A fast moult ensures that the birds will return to a normal state of health much more quickly than is the case in a slow moult, and, naturally, that is an ideal situation.

Having completed the training programme, the show season, which begins in June, will be upon us, and we must now begin to consider how to go about the process of preparing the birds, the show cages, and the entry of the birds. Before we discuss the preparation of the birds, however, and for the benefit of the beginner in particular, we must discuss the **Standard Show Cage**, which is very specific and built to very exact dimensions laid down by **The Budgerigar Society**. The beginner should also be made aware that this is the only type of show cage in which a Budgerigar can be exhibited under the rules of the Society.

THE STANDARD SHOW CAGE

Size: Overall measurements: 14 in. long, 12 in. high, $6\frac{1}{2}$ in wide. (35.56 cm x 30.48 cm x 16.51 cm.)

Wood: Top and bottom, $\frac{1}{4}$ inch (0.64 cm) finished; sides and false roof $\frac{5}{16}$ inch (0.79 cm), finished; in red or white deal, pine or redwood. Back, good 4 mm plywood nailed outside.

Door: (a) size: 4in. by $3\frac{1}{2}$in; (10.16 cm by 8.89 cm) (b) fasteners: one flat loop wire, 15 gauge, length $1\frac{1}{2}$in. (3.81 cm) outside, $1\frac{1}{4}$ inch (3.18 cm) inside, at bottom left hand of door, $\frac{3}{4}$ inch (1.91 cm) from left edge and $\frac{3}{4}$ inch (1.91 cm) from bottom edge. One plain brass desk turn, 1 inch (2.54 cm) long fixed above top left hand door in line with the loop wire fastener; (c) two strong brass hinges, 1 inch (2.54 cm) by $\frac{5}{8}$ inch (1.59 cm) (when open) at right hand side, fixed $\frac{3}{4}$ inch (1.91 cm) from top and bottom respectively; (d) to open $\frac{7}{8}$ inch (2.22 cm) wire S hook, 16 gauge in centre of door; (e) left hand edge, top and bottom of door, sloping bevel cut; right hand edge straight cut (to take hinges); $3\frac{3}{4}$ inch (9.53 cm) overall from cage bottom and centred with sides.

Figure 8.3 Standard Show Cage *Top:* Front view *Bottom:* Side with door
Courtesy The Budgerigar Society

Front Rail: (a) height $2\frac{3}{4}$ inch (6.99 cm) from cage floor, (b) thickness of wood $\frac{5}{16}$ inch (0.79 cm) finished; (c) pot fixed on removable door, $\frac{3}{8}$ inch (0.95 cm) by $\frac{3}{4}$ inch (1.91 cm) sloping bevel cut; door pull, $\frac{5}{8}$ inch (1.59 cm) wire S hook, 16 gauge.

Drinker: White plastic, $2\frac{1}{2}$ inch (6.35 cm) by $1\frac{1}{2}$ inch (3.81 cm) with $\frac{1}{4}$ inch (0.64 cm) flange at each end and $\frac{5}{8}$ inch (1.59 cm) deep.

Perches: (a) length $4\frac{1}{2}$ inch (11.43 cm) overall, diameter $\frac{9}{16}$ inch (1.43 cm) finished; ends flush cut, not pointed or cone-shaped; (b) plainboss at back projecting $\frac{1}{2}$ inch (1.27 cm) diameter, $1\frac{1}{4}$ inch (3.18 cm) not painted; (c) position: screw holes at back of cage to be $5\frac{1}{2}$ inch (13.97) from bottom, overall, and $\frac{3}{8}$ inch (0.95 cm) apart; perches at front then centre with the crossbar.

Wire Front: (a) comprises 21 wires, 14 gauge, mesh $\frac{5}{8}$ inch (1.59 cm) centre to centre (b) height of crossbar, $5\frac{1}{2}$ inch (13.97 cm) overall, i.e. including bottom of cage; (c) for strength, double punched, set $\frac{3}{8}$ inch apart; (d) curve at top, $\frac{3}{4}$ inch (1.91 cm) to bow; (e) fixing, three wires left as spikes at the top and bottom.

Top: (a) width approximately $5\frac{1}{2}$ inch (13.97 cm) sufficiently wide to cover strengthening bar; (b) hand hole, kidney shaped, $3\frac{1}{4}$ inch (8.26 cm) by $1\frac{1}{4}$ inch; (3.18 cm) (c) height of sloping false roof, $8\frac{1}{2}$ inch (21.59 cm) from floor of cage.

Colour: Inside and wire front, white; outside, black.

Name: No maker's name or mark must appear on the cage.

The standard **show cage** as described incorporates patent No 755106, and a small plastic slip with that information is placed at the top left hand corner of the drinker on the outside front of the cage.

STATUS

It is not reasonable for those who are inexperienced to be forced to show their birds in opposition to breeders who may have twenty or more years behind them in the fancy. This fact is recognised by **The Budgerigar Society**, and consequently, **Budgerigar Society** members are given status commensurate with the length of time they have been in the fancy, or until they have achieved success in that particular category before progressing upward to the next.

The newcomer will start at the bottom of the scale with the status of 'Beginner', and should then progress through 'Novice' and 'Intermediate' to 'Champion'. The words are printed in inverted commas, because in the context of **Budgerigar Society** rules, they have very specific meanings. Before entering his birds for a show held under **Budgerigar Society** rules, it is essential that the beginner should know, and understand them.

SHOW RULES

1. The colour feeding of Budgerigars is debarred; also the use of any preparation whatsoever which causes the birds in the slightest degree to show unnatural colour, or the specific use of agents for the sole purpose of promoting artificial growth. The trimming of wings and/or tail is also debarred and it is an offence to cut an official ring for the purpose of putting it on the leg of a Budgerigar and to exhibit a Budgerigar wearing more than one closed ring. The exhibition and sale of Budgerigars so treated is strictly forbidden and members showing or selling such birds render themselves liable to severe disciplinary action. Judges, and/or any member of the Executive Committee present, or the Secretary of the Show if there is neither a Member of the Executive Committee nor of the General Council present, may impound any bird and the cage in which it was exhibited which they consider has been faked or dyed in any way, or is wearing an unrecognised ring in breeders classes or is presented in any fraudulent or misleading manner whatsoever. In all cases of alleged dyeing, even though tests may be made at the show, the bird must be impounded and forwarded to the General Secretary of **The Budgerigar Society**. The judge or judges and/or any member of the Executive Committee, or the General Council, or the Secretary of the Show will give the exhibitor and the General Secretary of **The Budgerigar Society** notice of impounding by personal intimation or telegram immediately, and by registered post within seven days thereof, specifying the alleged offence. The impounded bird shall be immediately forwarded to the General Secretary of **The Budgerigar Society**, it being insured for £100. The judge, judges, or the member of the Executive Committee or of the General Council or the Secretary of the Show shall make a note in writing of the code number and serial number and year number from the bird's ring in the presence of witnesses to ensure identification. At the show and before the bird is actually impounded it shall be examined by the judges and/or members of the Executive Committee or General Council or the Show Secretary, who will forward their report to the Secretary of **The Budgerigar Society** who will take any action necessary thereon in accordance with the Society's rules. The Society or any of the officials concerned with the impounding of a bird will not be responsible for any loss sustained to the bird or otherwise during such impounding, and it shall remain impounded until such time as the investigations are complete and, if necessary, full disciplinary action taken.

1a. A judge's decision is final subject to show rule 1 but judges are instructed to consult other judges when in doubt regarding a particular exhibit before making a decision.

2. Special prizes offered by the Society shall only be competed for at Patronage Shows. Members must mark their entry forms **B.S.** Failure to do so debars the exhibitors from taking any **B.S** award, with the exception of Best in Show.

PARTNERSHIPS

3a. Any member of the Society who enters into a partnership or arrangement with any other member or members must give notice in writing to the Secretary, stating the names of the parties concerned in the partnership, and entry forms to show secretaries must be correctly worded, clearly showing that such exhibits are the joint property of the exhibitors concerned. Members of any partnership must exhibit solely in the section of the highest ranking member of the said partnership, and each member must be a paid up member of the Society. In the case of partnerships formed between the end of a breeding season and the start of a show season, a certificate may be obtained on request to allow the new partnership to exhibit current year birds wearing rings bearing the code number of either partner in the breeders classes for the first year only of the partnership. In the event of a partnership dissolving, a certificate may be obtained on request, from the General Secretary, by either partner to enable them to show partnership ringed birds in the breeders' classes under their own names for the remainder of the show season. Failure to observe these partnership regulations shall debar the allocation of all **B.S.** awards.

b. Where two or more exhibitors breed or keep their Budgerigars at one establishment, aviary or dwelling, such exhibitors must exhibit in the highest section as the said exhibitors. This rule also applies to Junior members.

4. February 28 shall be deemed to end the exhibition year. Thus a bird hatched at any time during the current year can compete as a young bird up to 28th February in the following year. All exhibits competing in Breeders' classes must have been bred by and wear the official coded closed ring of the actual exhibitors. No nomination is required for ring scheme awards.

5. All entries made by members at shows supported by the Society which are too late for printing in the printed or duplicated catalogue will be debarred from taking any Society awards.

6. No exhibit shall be eligible for any **Budgerigar Society** Special Prize at any Patronage Show unless it is itself a first prize winner in its class at the show concerned, except in the class where the first prize winner is awarded best in show or best in section. In this class, the second prize winner may compete for second best in show. If the winner of best in show is a certificate winner the runner up for that certificate should also be considered for second best in show when such a special is scheduled. (Show promoting societies are strongly urged to adopt this rule for their own specials in order to make the judges' task easier with regard to the Budgerigar Section.)

7. At all shows receiving the patronage of **The Budgerigar Society** exhibitors understand and agree that the managements and/or any member of the Executive Committee present at the show concerned is empowered to handle and examine exhibits in the Breeders classes if considered necessary.

8. The counting of points for **Budgerigar Society** special prizes at Patronage Shows shall be as follows: The seven highest awards in each class to count for points, first to count seven points. If less than seven exhibits, the first award shall count the same number of points as there are exhibits in the class. Each award after the first to count one point less than the award next above.

9. All exhibits must be shown in the standard **show cage** with the white ivorine plate on the front rail and no markings or labels other than the class label shall appear on the show cage front rail. The class label shall be centred on the front rail.

10. Floor of cages to be covered with any seed suitable for Budgerigars but millet sprays, whole or in part, shall not be permitted until after judging.

11. Judges officiating at shows held under the rules of the **B.S.** shall not be allowed to exhibit in the Budgerigar Section.

12. **Definition of Junior, Beginner, Novice and Intermediate**

Junior A junior paying a juvenile subscription must exhibit in Junior classes only but the best junior bird should be judged along with other birds for the best in show. In the case of championship shows it must first compete for best of its colour.

Beginner A beginner may exhibit in Beginners classes for three show seasons, or until he or she has won four first prizes in Beginner section in full classes in competition at open shows, whichever is the longer period.

Novice A novice may exhibit in novice classes for three show seasons, or until he or she has won four first prizes in Novice section in full classes in competition at open shows, whichever is the longer period.

129

Intermediate An intermediate may exhibit in intermediate classes for four show seasons, or until he or she has won six first prizes in Intermediate section in full classes in competition at open shows, whichever is the longer period.

Note I A full class shall be seven exhibits with not less than three exhibitors.

Note II A member who commences the season as a beginner, a novice or an intermediate may continue as such until the end of that show season, even if he or she has attained a higher status.

Note III Breeders classes and any age classes at open shows are considered **open** competition for the purpose of the above definition.

Note IV In the case or more than one member residing at the same address they shall each take the same status as the other, that being the highest status of any one of them. For example: if one is an intermediate and the other a novice, they must both show as intermediates. This condition does not apply to unrelated sub-tenants. Where two or more exhibitors breed or keep their Budgerigars at one establishment, aviary or dwelling, such exhibitors must exhibit in the highest section of the said exhibitors.

Note V If a bird wins a first in a class containing fewer than seven exhibits and not less than three exhibitors but then wins Best in Section, the win counts as a first prize in the application of wins conditions in the above definitions. (That such wins shall not count towards status unless there are not fewer than six exhibitors in the section.)

Note VI The status conditions commence from the first year a member exhibits. No allowance will be made for a break in continuity of exhibiting.

13. Any exhibitor may, if he or she desires, exhibit in a section higher than that of their present status, but having once done so (irrespective of not having been awarded a prize in the higher section) shall not be allowed to exhibit in a lower section at any future show, except that, in the case of intermediate or beginner exhibitors, at shows where no intermediate or beginner classes are scheduled, they may enter in the next higher section without losing their lower status. An exhibitor is not allowed to exhibit in more than one Budgerigar section.

Note I Birds kept at the residence of a person who has exhibited in a certain status cannot be shown by a new owner in a lower status.

14. No person under suspension shall be allowed to judge or exhibit at any show held under the rules of **The Budgerigar Society**.

15. All exhibits must be the bona fide property of the exhibitor.

16. A bird must not be exhibited under the person from whom it was purchased, nor under the breeder and a bird which has been bought must not be exhibited until it has been the property of the purchaser and in his keeping for not less than twenty-eight days.

17. Re-joining members: Any person who has been completely out of the fancy, and who has not owned or exhibited birds for a period of five years, on rejoining the **B.S.** can take one status lower than that which he enjoyed when he was previously a member of the **B.S.**

18. Members re-joining the Society can be issued with their old code numbers providing they are available and all back subscriptions paid up. The paying of back subscriptions does not, however, entitle members to qualify for the ten years unbroken membership in connection with the judges panel. Widows of members who wish to do so can apply for membership and have their husband's code number but they must also take his exhibitor status.

19. **Championship Shows** (Procedure) A judge will judge the best of his/her colour, which will go forward for the award of best in show. The best in show will be selected from the best bird of the 13 colours (which will include the best junior bird if it has been judged best of its colour). After best in show has been judged, it will be necessary to

ensure that the proposed certificate winners are wearing an official ring. If a bird judged the winner of a certificate is found to belong to a non-member of the **B.S.**, or not nominated **B.S.**, the bird second in its class should be considered for the award together with the next best in colour. Then the remainder of the specials will be judged and, finally, ring numbers of certificate winners must be checked and inserted on the certificate by the judge immediately on completion of all judging before he signs the certificate. Once a bird has been given an award of best in its colour it cannot thereafter be beaten by a bird of its colour for any other **B.S.** award.

These, then, are the conditions under which shows are held, and the beginner, even if he is not a member of **The Budgerigar Society**, which he is strongly advised to join, should study them very carefully before showing his birds.

There is one point which does sometimes cause a little confusion for the beginner, and that is the difference between an **Open Show** and a **Club Show**. If a show is advertised as an Open Show, then anyone may enter their birds, whether they are members of the organising club or not. A Club or Members' Show is confined to the members of the organising club, and unless one becomes a member of that club then entries will not be accepted.

NEST FEATHER SHOWS

Possibly the first show which a new fancier will attend will be a Nest Feather Show. This type of show is much less formal than the Open or Club Show, and is usually held on meeting nights in the club room. Despite the informality, and, at times, the rather loose interpretation of the rules, such shows will give a valuable insight to the beginner, preparing him for the time when he will enter for his first show held strictly to the rules. Entries are usually made on the night of the show when the birds are taken to the hall, and I believe it true to say that most fanciers do not go to the lengths of spraying or bathing their birds in the same methodical manner as they would for a larger show.

Such a show has another advantage to beginner and champion alike, in that this is the first time his birds will be up against competition, and this will allow a comparison to be made. From such shows, one can gain an impression of the state of advancement of one's own birds, and their quality in relation to the birds of the Champions and of other beginners who will probably be providing the opposition at the Club Shows or Open Shows in the area.

It has another advantage for the birds. Although this will not be a large show, they will be peered at, lifted up, examined, talked about and will generally come into close contact with a comparatively large body of people for the first time. It is very true that the birds learn a lot from

131

their first show, and are much steadier the second time out. In that sense, the Nest Feather Show provides very valuable experience for them.

Carrying the Birds to the Show

The following remarks apply to the transporting of birds to any show, whether Nest Feather or otherwise, and careful note must be taken.

Although Nest Feather Shows are usually held in May or June, no bird should ever be carried around outside in an Open Show cage. It is very probable that birds carried in this way at that time will suffer no harmful consequences, but that is certainly not the case in Winter or late Autumn. It is also possible of course, that even in May or June, it may be raining, and the bird may get wet on its way from the aviary to the car if the cage is not covered. It is then taken out of a warm car when the meeting hall is reached and carried in what are relatively cold conditions, remembering that the bird has wet feathers. It is then expected to sit for perhaps two or three hours in a cold meeting hall with another journey home before it is returned to the comfort of its own cage. The connotations of this set of circumstances are very obvious. What may not be so obvious is that in Winter, even carrying a bird for a few yards in an open cage can cause the bird to catch a chill which can then develop into something more serious and result in the loss of the bird.

The moral is clear. When taking birds to and from a show, make sure that they are taken in well constructed, solid carrying cases made to carry two, three or four show cages so that they are unable to move inside the case. Such a carrying case should have the name and address of the owner written clearly upon it in large letters, preferably painted on, and should be very securely fastened and have a good solid handle.

Most fanciers, for some inexplicable reason, paint their show cage carrying case black on the outside. In a crowded show hall, especially at an open show, this can cause problems if all the carrying cases are painted the same colour. A good idea is to paint the carrying cases a colour other than black, and then, on the ends, paint some distinguishing mark, a single wavy line or a square painted in a different colour to that of the carrying case. If this is done, one's own cases can be seen almost at a glance when they are stacked with others under the staging at the show hall.

Do not be afraid to turn up at the show hall with the birds in a cardboard box if there is nothing better. Most fanciers have done this from time to time, and most also know the expense involved in the initial setting up of a bird room. The beginner can be assured that the greater majority of fanciers know the feeling well, and accept that it is better to turn up with a box of any description rather than to risk losing a bird because one is too proud or some such silly reason. No one will pay any attention, but it should be pointed out that a good solid carrying case should be obtained or made as quickly as possible.

Preparing for the Show

Most breeders decide on which shows they will be entering before the start of the season, and usually, a list of Open Shows appears in *Cage and Aviary Birds*, the Fancy Press, at the appropriate time.

Beginners especially should note that it is very possible to over show a bird, and although, if one has bred what is usually referred to by fanciers as 'a stormer' — a very good show specimen — one must take care not to over tire the bird by showing it too often in any one season. This applies particularly because it is not reasonable to expect a bird to be shown every week, going through the whole rigorous process, and still maintain its general health and brightness so it continues to win. Equally, it is not reasonable to show such a bird and, soon after the show season, begin breeding operations.

It is usually considered that five two-day Open Shows are quite enough for one bird in any given season, although one-day Club Shows can be discounted.

Having decided upon which of the shows are being entered, the next step is to wait for the announcement of the show to appear in the press, and to send for the show schedule, which should be applied for immediately the show announcement appears. That will allow more time for the fancier to make up his mind which of his birds are to be entered and in which classes.

The Show Schedule

The show classification, the schedule, is usually made out in the following manner.

Any Age Classes					**Breeders Classes**			
Ch.	Int	Nov	Beg		Ch.	Int	Nov	Beg
1	37	73	109	Light, Dark or Olive Green Cock	19	55	91	127
2	38	74	110	Light, Dark or Olive Green Hen	20	56	92	128
3	39	75	111	Sky, Cobalt, Mauve or Violet Cock	21	57	93	129
4	40	76	112	Sky, Cobalt, Mauve or Violet Hen	22	58	94	130
5	41	77	113	Grey or Greygreen Cock	23	59	95	131
6	42	78	114	Grey or Greygreen Hen	24	50	96	132
7	43	79	115	Opaline Green Cock	25	61	97	133
8	44	80	116	Opaline Green Hen	26	62	98	134
9	45	·81	117	Opaline Blue Cock	27	63	99	135
10	46	82	118	Opaline Blue Hen	28	64	100	136

On close examination, it is apparent that this is the logical progression for classification. The beginner will no doubt note that the classification runs from **Champion Any Age**, through **Champion Breeders**, then on to the **Intermediate Section** and so on.

One of the most common mistakes is for birds to be entered in the wrong age group, that is, birds which should be entered in the breeders' classes being entered in the Any Age Class, and although there is nothing in the show rules of **The Budgerigar Society** to prevent this, it is an offence to enter an adult bird in the breeders' classes. Great care should be taken to avoid this type of mistake.

It is advisable that the schedule is obtained in plenty of time before the show, so that it can be filled in at leisure. Most mistakes on entry forms are made because the fancier was in a rush, and show secretaries do not take kindly to being asked to rectify mistakes on the morning of the show. In fact the rules usually state quite clearly that mistakes cannot be rectified after the closing date for entries.

The importance of making correct entries is, therefore, self evident. Make sure that the date of the show, the venue, the time at which birds can be taken to the hall, (usually either late on the night before the show or early on the morning of the show), the closing date for entries, the time for picking up one's birds after the show and all relevant details are clearly understood. Careful attention to these points will help to ensure that the fancier does not attend the show after judging only to find W/C written on the cage label by the judge, signifying that the bird has been entered in the wrong class.

Nominations

On the entry form, a space will be provided under the heading of Nominations. This is provided for members of the specialist societies, for example, **The Budgerigar Society**, and in the schedule, a code will be found with letters given for each specialist society.

The specialist societies usually put on what are termed 'Specials', for competition between the members of those societies. For example, one may find that the **Clearwing Society** is providing a special prize for the best Clearwing, and members of this society must put on the entry form the correct code letter in the space provided. Failure to do so may result in the breeder losing his special prize, even if his bird should be judged the best exhibit covered by that particular society.

The beginner should take advice from more experienced fanciers if he is in any doubt at all about which bird should be entered in which class. There is little point in going to all the trouble of show training, preparing the bird and its cage meticulously and then negating all one's hard work purely because the actual entry of the birds has been rushed, or because a chance has been taken on the bird being entered in the correct class.

CHOOSING THE TEAM

When choosing the birds which will, hopefully, prove to be winners during the coming show season, it is better to have a second string. For each bird which it is intended to enter, a runner up of the same type should be chosen, and should be put through the same training routine as the birds which are the first choice.

Frequently, one enters one's bird room to cage the birds ready for the show the next day, only to find that the best bird has shed a spot, or a tail feather. In such a case, there is only one thing to be done, and that is to substitute another bird of similar type and colour.

The exercise of choosing the show team should be carried out at the beginning of May so that the birds are ready for the shows in early July. This preparation period of eight weeks is essential but the timing will depend upon the date of the first show which the fancier intends to enter. If, for example, the first show is not until the beginning of August, then the exercise need not be carried out until the beginning of June. Eight weeks should be allowed, however, between choosing the team and the date of the first show. This will enable the fancier, if he chooses, to pull out the tail feathers and spots of the birds, giving them plenty of time to grow back before the show, and ensuring that the birds will not drop either tail or spot feathers in the few days before they are being put on exhibition.

REMOVING TAILS, SPOTS AND FLIGHTS

At this point, eight weeks before the first show, many fanciers remove the tails of the show team, together with any flight feathers which may be broken. This method ensures that the birds will have perfect tails and flights, and that the situation referred to above is avoided.

Spot feathers should be removed four weeks before a show. As with the tails and flights of the birds, pulling the spots will ensure that they have good masks when the show date arrives.

The tails and flights take eight weeks to grow out, and the spots will take four weeks. It is sometimes said that three weeks is the length of time for spots to grow and six weeks for tails, but occasionally these periods of time are extended, and it is better to allow a little longer to make sure.

When pulling tail or flight feathers, take them out singly. Trying to pull out the whole of the tail or two or more flights together will probably cause excessive pain to the bird, and may damage the bird

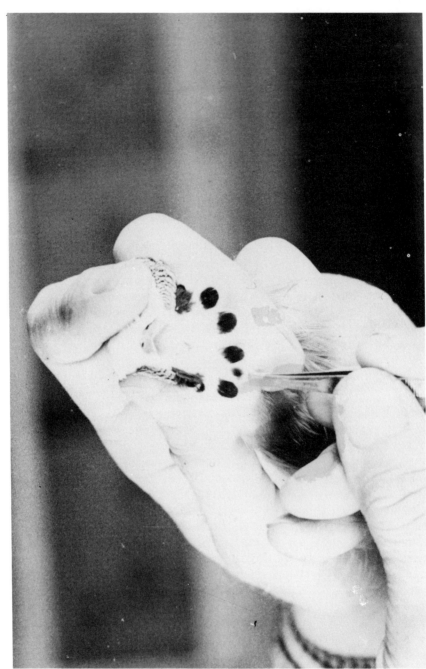

Figure 8.4 Before taking the Bird to a Show, the Mask should be trimmed and excess Spots removed

itself. Take a firm grip on the feather, and pull it quickly, the bird will feel little or no pain, but if one tries to pull the feather slowly, some distress may be caused.

When the spots are being pulled for show purposes, only the six large spots should be removed. There is no point in removing the flecking from the mask or any excess large spots since these will only grow again before the show date and will have to be removed again.

For this exercise, a pair of ladies eyebrow tweezers will be required, of the type with a squared, flat jaw. Pointed or angled types are not suitable. The fancier should make sure when buying tweezers for the purpose of trimming spots, that the jaws close perfectly at the ends by closing the ends and holding the tweezers edgeway to the light. The best ones to choose are those which come into contact for at least $\frac{1}{4}$ inch at the tips, thus ensuring a good grip on the feather. Those which touch only at the very tip should be discarded.

Many birds will be found to be double spotted, that is, they will have one spot growing over the top of another. In this case, the correct spot to remove is the bottom spot, leaving the top one in situ. For the purposes we are considering here, however, it is the top spot which should be removed, since this is the one we wish the bird to have for the show.

Assuming that the fancier is right handed, the bird should be taken up in the left hand and held in the correct manner. With the end of the tweezers closed, separate the spot from the one beneath and from the small feathers immediately surrounding it. Blowing on the feathers will help to separate the spotted feather, and when the edge of the feather is clearly separated, slip the bottom side of the tweezers underneath and close the tweezers together. At this point, move the spot around slightly with the tweezers without pulling, to make sure that the feather between the jaws is the one which needs to be pulled. Make sure that the tweezers have a firm grip, and give a quick pull, and the spot will come away very easily.

Spraying

As soon as the birds are chosen for showing, spraying should begin. Every day for two weeks, the birds should be heavily sprayed with a garden hand spray, using reasonably hot water. Some fanciers also use plume spray added to the water, but whether this is necessary at this point is a matter for personal choice.

When the birds are being sprayed, place four in an old show cage, or better still, an old Border Canary or Yorkshire Show cage if one can be obtained. Such cages are made entirely from wire, and the birds can be sprayed from any angle, as opposed to being sprayed only from the front if a Budgerigar Show Cage is used. The birds should be thoroughly soaked until the water is running from them and then returned to a spare stock cage in which clean sawdust has been placed, to dry out. A good method of carrying out this particular method of drying is to keep one section of a length of stock cages empty. When the birds are dry, simply remove the slide, allow the birds back into the stock cage and replace the slide ready for the drying cage to be used next day.

This operation is best carried out as early as possible during the day, and should not be carried out after about 2 p.m. Spraying too late in the day may result in the birds going to roost with their feathers damp; consequently they may catch a chill or perhaps worse.

After the first two weeks, the birds should only be sprayed every other day, and when there are only three weeks before the show, only light spraying every other day should be necessary. Usually, this will ensure that all extraneous dirt has been washed from the feathers, and giving only light sprays later will remove the day to day accumulation of dirt on the feathers.

Three days before the show, all spraying should cease. The feathers, when they are in good condition should have a silken sheen on them, and spraying in the manner described will remove the oil which gives this silky appearance. It will take the bird three days to replace the oil, and thus, the sheen.

When spraying has been stopped, the birds should be placed in clean stock cages with clean sawdust on the floors to help ensure that they do not soil their feathers at the last minute.

Trimming the Mask

Three days before the show, the masks of the birds should be trimmed by plucking the flecking and excess spots. Pluck each feather as described previously, and start with the small flecks. When the flecks have been trimmed, attend to the large spots. Remember that it is the lower spot which should be trimmed in cases where birds carry double spots. Spots should be plucked, and not cut. Some fanciers do cut unwanted flecks or spots with a small pair of nail scissors, but this leaves a straight edged feather which will almost certainly be more noticeable than if the spot is plucked as suggested.

Straighten the Tail

At the same time that the bird is being prepared for placing in its show cage, which would be the night before the show, the tail should be straightened by dipping it in hot water and running the feathers between the finger and thumb.

138

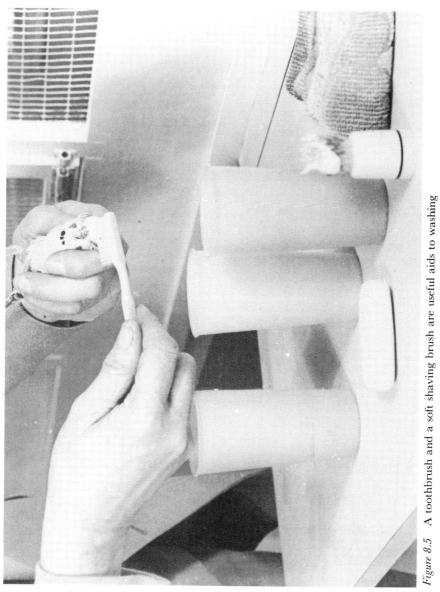

Figure 8.5 A toothbrush and a soft shaving brush are useful aids to washing

HAND WASHING

The methods given above should suffice in most cases and should ensure that the birds are clean, well trimmed and well presented for the show but, in some cases, hand washing may be necessary. It should be pointed out, however, that many fanciers do not believe in washing their birds by hand, and rely solely on spraying in order to have their birds sufficiently clean. Should a bird become too dirty, hand washing may be carried out, but this should not be done less than two weeks before the show. If birds are hand washed, then all of the natural oils will be washed out of the feathers, and will take appreciably longer to replace.

Before starting the procedure, three bowls of water, some baby soap, an old shaving brush and a thick towel should be prepared. Like spraying, hand washing should be carried out early in the day for the reasons previously explained.

The bird is taken in the hand in the normal manner, and the water is put on the body with the shaving brush. When the body is thoroughly wet, work up a lather with the brush and apply the soap to the bird. When the body is well lathered, work the lather into the feathers, again using the brush. When the body has been lathered, push the tips of the fingers under each wing in turn, which will give a firm surface and the lather can then be worked into the wings. If the bird is held so that the tail is pointing up the wrist, this will give a firm surface, and the tail can then receive the same treatment.

When the body, wings and tail have been treated, the head can be given attention. Care must be taken to see that lather does not run into the eyes, and the brush should not be too wet. Always brush backward, away from the face in the direction in which the feathers are growing, over the top of the head. Having washed the head, the mask should receive similar treatment, taking care to brush only in the direction in which the feathers are growing.

When the whole of the bird has been well lathered, the bird can be thoroughly rinsed in the second bowl of warm water, the same care being taken to see that the rinsing water does not carry lather into the eyes of the bird. Having rinsed the bird thoroughly, a second rinse is used to make sure that all of the soap has been washed out of the feathers. Some fanciers add a teaspoon of vinegar to the final rinsing water which helps to get rid of any excess suds.

After the final rinse, the bird should be wrapped in a rolled up towel with its head protruding and placed near a source of heat. Most fanciers place their birds on the mantel shelf above the fire for the drying process, but no matter where the bird is placed, care should be taken to ensure that it is not allowed to become too hot and uncomfortable. As the bird

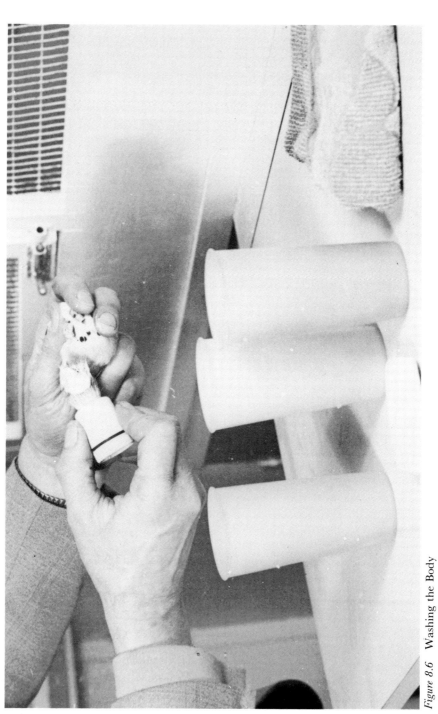

Figure 8.6 Washing the Body

begins to dry out, it is gradually moved further away from the fire, and after about two hours it should be sufficiently dry to be placed in a clean show cage in the living room to complete the drying process.

After washing is completed, the bird should not be replaced in the bird room immediately, but should be gradually moved from the warmth of the living room to a somewhat cooler room. Taking the bird from a very warm room straight back to the bird room, perhaps with damp feathers, will almost certainly cause chills and may even result in the death of the bird from respiratory disease.

Many fanciers do not believe in hand washing Budgerigars, and if the methods of spraying as described above are used, then there should really be no reason for the birds being so dirty as to need any further washing.

TAKING THE BIRDS TO THE SHOW

Birds can usually be taken to the show hall either on the evening of the day before the show, or early on the morning of the show day. I believe that it is true to say that most fanciers would prefer to take their birds to the show hall on the evening of the day before the show. The theory behind the preference for this practice is that when the birds are taken from their carrying case, possibly after a journey of two hours or more, if long distances have to be covered, they are not at their best if they are suddenly taken from almost pitch darkness into light, and what is more, into a totally strange environment.

If the bird is taken to the show hall on the morning of the show, it may well be that it will not have sufficient time to settle down and become accustomed to its new surroundings before it is placed on the Judge's bench and expected to behave impeccably. If, on the other hand, the bird is taken to the hall on the night before the show, it will have much more time to settle down, and will almost certainly be more amenable to 'performing' for the Judge. If circumstances do not allow this then the birds should be taken to the hall as early as possible on the day of the show for the reasons already stated.

Booking In

On reaching the show hall, the Show Secretary or the Section Secretary and their stewards will take the birds, check the entry form against their books, and will attend to the birds from that point on. The show rules do not allow for anyone, other than Judges and Officials, to be present in the hall during judging, and having handed over his birds, the exhibitor must then leave the hall.

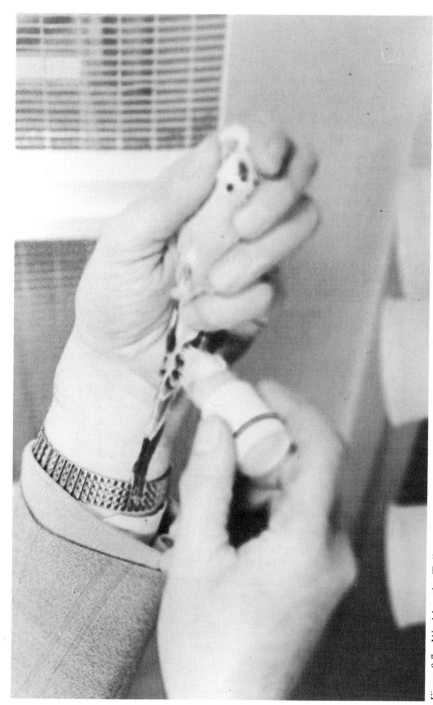

Figure 8.7 Washing the Tail

Cage Labels

The cage labels will have been sent by post well before the show date, and should be placed on the front of the cage in the centre of the bottom front as described in the show cage specification. Care must be taken here. It is by no means unknown for an exhibitor to reach the show hall, only to find that he has managed to switch two labels, and to find, for example, that the cage label pertaining to a normal green bird is on a cage containing an opaline green. If this situation occurs after the birds have been handed over to the stewards, then both birds would be considered to be incorrectly classed and would not be judged.

The best method of ensuring that mistakes of this nature do not occur is to place the birds in the cages before the labels are put on. Then, check the type and colour of the bird against the schedule and find out which class is appropriate. Find the correct class label and fix it to the cage, and the job is done. This particular point may appear to be somewhat superfluous, but beginners especially should note that putting the wrong label on a cage is a very common error, and one which is not always made by beginners!

JUDGING

The Judge will be asked to make his decision on which bird is the best in its class in the first instance. Following this, he will begin to choose the birds which will go forward for the special awards, including the Best in Show.

This is done by a process of elimination in the following manner. First, he will choose his best green from the green classes, and the best opposite sex. Then, the best blue and so on. Having chosen these birds, he will take all the birds chosen, and from these he will find the best cock and the best hen. The best of the two birds will become the Best in Show and the other the best opposite sex. This is perhaps an over simplification, especially in view of the numbers of special prizes which are awarded, particularly at Open Shows. There may be, for example, special prizes for the Best Cinnamon Marked Bird, and that particular winner will come from the first prize winners of all of the cinnamon classes. There may be a special prize for the Best Bird shown by a member of a particular society, and for that prize, the Judge will take all the first prize winners shown by members of that society and choose the best, if, that is, the Best Bird in Show owner is not a member.

This is the basic method of judging the birds, but it is not nearly so simple as it sounds. Judges are frequently confronted by birds which are very close together on points, and equally frequently they must make up their minds, favouring one bird over another for some minute difference.

144

Figure 8.8   Washing the Wings

Figure 8.9   The Washed Bird drying out in a Show Cage

After the Judging

After the birds have been judged, and the public are allowed into the hall, the beginner can do no better than to seek out the Judge and to ask about his own birds. By far the greater majority of Judges are very happy indeed to discuss the birds with beginners; to point out their faults or good points, and usually they are quite prepared to give the reasons for their choice.

Beginners should take note, however, that in all matters concerning the judging of Budgerigars, the decision of the Judge is final, and Judges do not take kindly to argument. A Judge is employed for one purpose, and for one purpose only, and that is to give an honest and considered opinion, with special emphasis on the word opinion. No two Judges will see the same bird in the same manner, and it is incumbent upon fanciers to accept the Judge's decision gracefully, even though they may not necessarily agree with that decision. If a Judge has given his decision fairly and honestly, then that is all that should be expected of him. In any event, there is little point in arguing with the Judge because once the decision has been made, nothing will change it. Apart from which, arguing with a Judge and questioning his opinion is very rude and should not even be considered.

Asking the Judge's opinion of one's birds is quite a different matter, however, and the beginner will, if he uses his eyes and his ears, be able to learn a great deal about his own birds and about birds in general if he listens to these very experienced fanciers.

ATTENTION TO DETAIL

Success on the show bench is often achieved by the fancier who pays attention to detail. First, make sure that the bird is entered in the correct class. Second, prepare the birds and their show cages as meticulously as possible. Third, make sure that the correct label is on the cage to match the bird, and fourth and most important, make absolutely sure that the bird which is placed in a show cage is fit and well and in the peak of condition. Attention to these details may mean the difference between success and failure. Remember always that the bird is only able to do what its natural qualities will allow. It is up to the exhibitor to do the rest and to give the bird the best possible chance.

147

CHAPTER 9

GENETICS

OUT CROSSING AND LINE BREEDING

Before setting out to establish a stud of Budgerigars which will consistently produce exhibition stock which are equal to, or better than the parents, a knowledge of genetics — mechanics by which young are produced — is necessary. Without at least some knowledge of the manner in which good and bad points are passed from parent to offspring, there is little chance of the beginner achieving success in the establishment of a true breeding strain, except perhaps by chance, which is undoubtedly possible, but highly unlikely. Good exhibition birds have been bred from parents which have not in themselves carried good exhibition points, but since such birds would be extremely unlikely to produce young carrying all their good points, the beginner should discount such matters and should rely totally on his knowledge of the genetic make up of his stock.

PRODUCTION OF SEX CELLS

All living creatures are made up of millions of cells of one type or another. In the body tissues, these cells wear out and regenerate themselves, but the production of the sex cells is a quite different matter.

In each cell are two sets of chromosomes, tiny particles of matter, which have even more minute particles superimposed upon them, which are called genes. It is the genes which will determine such matters as colour, size, the size and number of spots and so on. From the sex cells of each parent, the offspring will inherit one half of the chromosomes, which are present in pairs within the cell. The manner in which this operates is really very simple.

When sex cells are being formed the normal cell divides, with a wall forming between the two halves, thus creating what might be termed

148

two half cells. This, of course, applies to both the cock and the hen. At this point, therefore, we have four half cells, each containing a half set of chromosomes.

The half cells are then united when the sperm from the cock penetrates the ovum of the hen. We then have whole cells again, each containing a full set of chromosomes, but the new cells now contain a half set of chromosomes from each parent. This can perhaps be explained more clearly in diagramatic form as follows:

COCK   HEN

XX		YY
XX		YY
XX		YY
XX		YY

THE WHOLE CELLS THEN DIVIDE INTO:

X	X		Y	Y
X	X		Y	Y
X	X		Y	Y
X	X		Y	Y

THEY THEN REUNITE ON FERTILISATION TO:

XY		XY
XY		XY
XY		XY
XY		XY

This is a very much simplified version of what actually occurs, but for the present, it serves to illustrate the point.

From this it can clearly be seen that the offspring take one half of their genetic make up, their genotype, from each of their parents. Let us now progress a step further. Suppose that one has, on one hand, a very good cock in terms of visual quality, its phenotype, but more importantly for present purposes, of good genotype, and a hen which has a poor phenotype and poor genotype. Let us further suppose that the cock has a particularly good head, and that the object of the exercise is to produce offspring with good heads.

When the sex cells are being produced, there are many hundreds concerned in one act of mating, and from those, the question of which cell containing the good genetic factors from the cock combines with which cell containing the good factors from the hen is purely a matter of chance. Therefore, unless both birds have a good genetic make up, the chances of their good points combining in the new cell are remote. In the case of the two birds we are now discussing, the chances of producing good offspring are extremely remote.

From the example given, it is clear that breeding from birds which do not have a good genotype is not the way to produce a line of true breeding stock.

As a general rule, it is better to breed from birds which also have good visual qualities, that is, a good phenotype. Such birds must, by very virtue of their appearance carry the genetic quality which is necessary to give them a good phenotype, in the sense that if a bird does not have a good gene for the production of large spots, and is mated with a similar bird, then in no way can the pair produce young with large spots. Conversely, if the bird carries large spots, then patently it must have that factor present in its genotype. If such a bird is mated to a similar bird then the chances of their producing young with large spots are much greater.

DOMINANT AND RECESSIVE GENES

Having progressed thus far, we must now understand that some genes are dominant to others. For example, the gene which gives the colour green, is dominant to all others, and, therefore, if two genes come together in the same fertilised ovum, one carrying green, the other carrying another colour, then the result of that particular combination will be green offspring.

It is possible, however, for a bird to carry the green gene, the dominant gene, which gives it its green colour, but also to carry the gene for blue. In such cases, the blue gene is termed recessive, and such a bird would be referred to as being green split for blue and written Green/Blue.

Diagrammatically the result of such a pairing with a true breeding, (homozygous) blue bird, that is, one which carries two blue genes, would be:

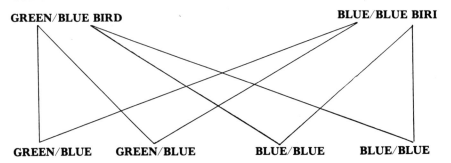

GREEN/BLUE BIRD			BLUE/BLUE BIRI
GREEN/BLUE	GREEN/BLUE	BLUE/BLUE	BLUE/BLUE

Again, note that half of the genes come from the cock, the other half from the hen, and also bear in mind that green is dominant to blue. We therefore have from the above mating, 50 per cent green birds because of the dominance of the green character but which carry the recessive blue from their mother. The other 50 per cent of the offspring will be blue, having inherited only blue from the hen, and the recessive blue gene from the cock. The Green/Blue offspring will be capable of producing both green and blue young if mated again to blue birds, but the blue/blue will be able to produce only blue/blue young birds if a similar pairing is made.

The beginner especially should be made aware, however, that there are very few birds today which are not split for some other colour.

INDETERMINATE GENES

While the genes for colour can be classified as being dominant or recessive, there are other genetic factors which cannot be so classified. Remembering that the appearance of the young is brought about by a combination of factors present on the chromosomes, and as a direct result of the combining of those factors we may have, on the one hand, a hen with large spots and a cock with small spots, the object of breeding the two together being to produce young with large spots.

The genes for large or small spots will combine in the fertilised ovum, but the outcome of such a combination is not so clearly defined as that in which the dominance of a particular gene is known. The resulting chick may have large or small spots, because the genes which give it its appearance are of an indeterminate character. The same process applies to head size, wing carriage and so on.

Because of the indeterminate character of these types of gene, the outcome of the mating of two birds of unknown genotype can only be a matter of chance, no matter what anyone else may say. There is, however, a method which will allow the breeder to know precisely what the outcome of a particular mating will be, namely, the process of what is known as line breeding.

There can be no question but that this is the only method by which a true breeding line can be established, and when such a line of sound true to type birds has been established, and it comes to a question of exhibition, the birds from such a stud will, as they say, take some beating.

LINE BREEDING

The object of line breeding is to establish a strain of birds which will

151

consistently produce good show stock if paired to others of the same family which have a similar genetic make up. In order to achieve this state of affairs, those genetic features which produce the less desirable features of an exhibition Budgerigar will have to be selectively eradicated. It should be remembered that the emphasis is not so much on the establishing of good points, but upon the elimination of the undesirable.

The eradication of the bad points and the establishment of the good can be described diagramatically, but before progressing further, and although not wishing to labour the point, the reader should remember that half of the genetic make up is taken from the cock and half from the hen. The resulting genetic make up of the offspring is, therefore, a combination of half of the genetic make up of each of the parent birds.

Having established that fact let us now consider the breeding stock. No breeder will sell a bird which presents visually all of the desirable points of an exhibition Budgerigar, even though it may not have the necessary genotype to reproduce its mirror image. Such a bird, although it may not be kept for breeding purposes, will be a good exhibition specimen, and will be kept for that reason. This being so, it follows that if the fancier has a bird which is like that described, but also has the genetic desirability, then no amount of money will be sufficient. Therefore, it also follows that the beginner will have to make a start with birds which have faults, and, what is more important, will also carry those faults in their genetic make up, probably along with others of a recessive nature.

The theory behind this will be demonstrated in a moment, but let it be quite clear that no fancier is about to sell line bred stock which has taken many seasons to establish, coupled with many years of breeding experience, and its attendant disappointments. The beginner must therefore choose the best birds which are available, with the fewest possible faults, and will then have to set about breeding his own line of birds.

Let us now examine the theory of line breeding, taking it stage by stage from fault carrying stock and discuss how we are to go about eliminating these faults.

First, let us assume that the initial cock and hen have good heads. In my view, this is essential because lack of head size, especially lack of height over the back skull and breadth between the eyes, are probably the most difficult desirable points to breed into a line, and I would not advise the beginner to start with birds which do not have these desirable traits.

We will then assume, that the cock has good spots, but carries a gene for small spots, while the hen has small spots, but carries the gene for large. The cock is assumed to be on the small side, as also is the hen, but both carry the genes for the production of larger offspring.

We will assume that the hen has a good tail carriage, while the cock has not such a good carriage, but carries the invisible ability to reproduce such a carriage in his offspring. In the following diagrams, the good points are represented by capitals and the bad points by small letters. **H** for **head size**; **SP** for **spots**; **S** for **overall size**, and **T** for **tail and wing carriage**.

Taking our two parent birds then, and again, remembering that they will have inherited half their genetic make up from each of their parents, we have:

```
        COCK                    HEN
        H  H                    H  H
        SP sp                   sp SP
         s  S                    s  S
         t  T                    T  T
```

The cells will then divide and on mating would produce four half cells as previously described to give the following combinations;

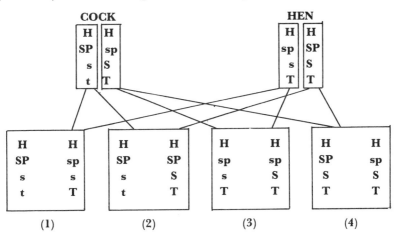

From the division of whole cells to half cells and the recombining of these, we now find that we have four distinctly different birds, in genetic terms at least.

Bird number one will have a good head, but may or may not have a good tail carriage, spots or size. Bird number three will have a good head and a good tail carriage, and while it may or may not be of good size, it will almost certainly carry small spots. Bird number two will possibly carry all the desirable features for which we are aiming, but probably the best of our four mythical birds would be number four, which with the exception of a gene for small spots from the cock, has inherited a genetic make up which is very close to the required standard.

This, then, is the theory behind the production of a strain of birds which carry a good genotype, whether it always works in practice is, of course, quite a different matter. Whether bird number four will or will not have good spots is largely a matter of chance, but in the example given, and assuming that the breeder knows the genotype of the parents, the chances of producing such a bird which shows all the desirable points are far greater than would otherwise be the case.

It should now be equally clear that unless the genetic make up of the parent birds is known, there is little point in breeding from a pair of birds on purely visual grounds. If the genes for the desirable points are not present, then there is no possible chance of producing birds which will carry those points visually.

It is for this reason that the newcomer to breeding should ask to see the parents, and if possible the grandparents of the birds he intends to buy. If the antecedents of the birds concerned are of equal quality to their descendants, then it can be assumed that line breeding has been involved, and the outcome of the exercise can be predicted with reasonable accuracy.

Again, this is also the reason for the beginner being advised to purchase his initial breeding stock from the champion breeders, since his stock will almost certainly be line bred.

Having some knowledge of the manner in which genetic inheritance takes place, we must now consider how we may put that knowledge to use in order to fix the desirable points into our stud.

ESTABLISHING THE LINE

Line breeding, or, as it is sometimes known, inbreeding, is quite a simple operation in theory, and consists simply of mating the best cock from a given pair back to the hen, its mother, and the best hen back to its father. If we examine the theory in diagrammatic terms, the reasons behind the theory become quite clear, and, basically, they are sound.

Let us assume that the fourth bird from the previous diagram is a cock and that the second bird is a hen. Diagrammatically, we then have:

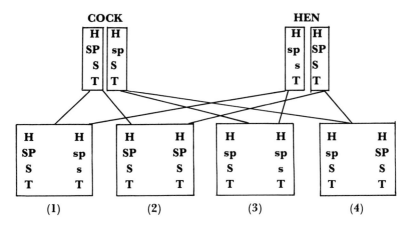

From this pairing of son to mother, we now have one bird with the same genetic make up as its father, bird number four, and another with the same genetic make up as its mother, bird number one. In addition, and far more importantly, we have a bird which carries the pure genetic make up which we require in bird number two. We have now reached the stage at which the sex of this particular bird is immaterial, but, for our purposes, we will assume that it is a hen. This hen is bred back to its father, and we now have:

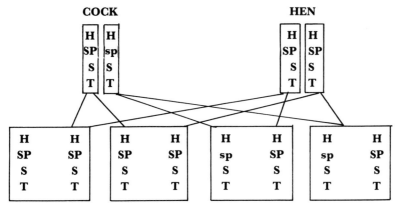

From this pairing, we have two birds which carry the desirable visual qualities, and these two birds should be paired back to their grandparents, both of which have the genetic make up which is required to produce young of the required standard. Logically, it would be more reasonable to breed the birds back to their parents, but inbreeding too closely produces a weaker strain in general terms, and is not to be desired if the situation can be avoided.

155

From the diagrams a logical progression can be seen, and when the last stage is reached as described, it follows that all one needs to do to carry on consistently producing birds of the desired type, is to carry on breeding grandson back to grandmother or granddaughter back to grandfather.

In all of this, one factor which must be considered is the age of the hen at the point at which the line is begun. Budgerigar hens are usually considered, in my view correctly, to be past their best for breeding purposes after they have reached the age of three years. If we accept this as being correct, then unless a hen is used as the foundation of a line during her first breeding season, then there is little possibility of carrying out the exercise as set down here. Recent evidence suggests that Budgerigar hens are being used for breeding purposes when they are past their prime, and there is a suggestion that this may also be a cause of infertility. Whether or not that is correct is still a matter for conjecture, but certainly the scientific evidence is beginning to indicate that such is the case. If and when the point is proved, then the age of the breeding hen will assume even greater importance than it does at present and will in all probability lead to even greater problems for the serious breeder. If, as I believe, the point will be proved, then this will inevitably lead to other problems related to genetic inheritance so far as the line breeder is concerned.

PROGENY TESTING

From the diagrams, it can be clearly seen that a given bird may carry, for example, large spots, but may also carry the gene for small spots. The only way in which one can be certain of whether the bird carries a gene from each of its parents for large spots, or whether it carries one gene for large and one for small, is to breed the bird with another which is known to carry genes which will produce the large spots.

If the bird which is an unknown quantity is bred to one, the genetic make up of which is known, then two things may happen. Either the offspring will all carry large spots, in which case the bird of unknown attributes will have been proved as far as is reasonably possible to carry the double gene for large spots, or some of the offspring will have large spots and others small spots, in which case the bird carries one desirable attribute and one which is not desirable.

This experiment will undoubtedly allow the breeder to know what he may or may not expect of the bird in question, but if the experiment is carried out, then an entire breeding season has been lost if the bird turns out to be carrying the undesirable attribute. It is at this point that luck enters the arena.

156

Referring again to the diagrams, we see that some birds will carry a true breeding genotype, while others may well present the desirable visual qualities, but will also have in their genetic make up the ability to reproduce undesirable qualities. How, then, is the breeder to know the difference if both birds are visually equal? The short answer is that one cannot; not, that is, without going through the process of progeny testing with a bird of known breeding quality. In such a case, and bearing in mind the relatively short breeding life, especially of the hens, one can only take a chance and hope that one has made the correct choice.

There is a very great danger here, because if the bird from the two which exhibit the desirable qualities happens to be the one which carried a mixed genetic make up then, by breeding this bird back to its grandparent, one is simply breeding back into the line one of the qualities which it was intended should be eliminated.

The outcome of this process, or rather the extent of the effect, can however be offset to some degree. Obviously the bird with the undesirable genetic make up will show that feature in its progeny, and the following season, the bird which carries the desirable points can be bred back to its grandparent and the line continued. Either way, only one breeding season has been lost.

CONTINUING THE LINE

So far, we have considered using only the best cock and the best hen from a mating of father to daughter in the first instance from the original pair, or son to mother as the case may be. The question now arises, what of the other chicks?

Remembering what was said in the chapter on stock selection concerning the purchase of four good pairs; treating each pair in the same manner, and of course, assuming that both pairs have a good genetic background — possibly even the same genotype if they have been bought from a single supplier — it is possible to have three separate blood lines running alongside each other after the first breeding season.

After deciding which of the first generation chicks are preferred for breeding back to their parents, the second best cock and hen are chosen from each pair, thus giving six breeding pairs.

It is at this point that many beginners make a cardinal error. The beginner is prone to believing that every available inch of space in the bird room should be filled with breeding cages, and that every cage should be occupied by a breeding pair. If the object is to establish a true breeding line, then under no circumstances should any bird lower down the scale than second best in any given nest be used for breeding purposes. As we have seen, such birds carry undesirable points, and

157

these will be bred back into the line if these birds are used to perpetuate it.

Birds other than the best or second best from any pairing should be discarded and sold, and those which kept should be used in the following manner. For purposes of clarity we will consider only one pair, but, of course, the offspring from each of the original two pairs should be used in precisely the same manner.

From the offspring of the original pair, the best son and best daughter should be bred back to the mother and father respectively. The offspring of this mating, again the best son and best daughter, should be bred back to the original pair. The offspring of this pairing should then be bred back to the second generation birds; that is, those which were produced from the original pair. From the third generation onward, the second best cock and the second best hen should be bred back to their parents, while the best cock and the best hen continue to be mated back to their grandparents.

In theory, it should be possible to produce birds in the fourth generation which have a better genotype than the original pairs, and, perhaps more importantly for show purposes, a better phenotype.

Having noted all of this, it must surely now be very clear that the quality of the original breeding pairs is of extreme importance, and the reasons for the purchase of such birds from an established line bred stud should be equally clear. Theoretically, it is possible to eventually evolve a stud of birds of both good genotype and good phenotype from birds which carry every fault possible by judicious elimination of birds carrying more faults than others. Unquestionably this can be done, but it would take many years. By the same token, the beginner must not believe that all one needs to do is to buy a pair of exceptionally good birds, thereby achieving instant success.

Luck certainly plays a large part in the overall scheme. For example, we have assumed that from the original pairing, the birds carrying the desirable qualities will be a cock and a hen, allowing us to breed son to mother and father to daughter. In practice, however, it may be that the two birds may be of the same sex and one may therefore have to use the second best bird for perpetuation of the line, thus, effectively adding another breeding season, and another year to the breeding programme before the desired outcome of the whole breeding scheme is reached. It may be that if one loses a chick through accident in the nest, this will be one of those which is required to carry on the line, and in such cases one can only make do with second best. These, and many other problems, will be encountered, and when they are one can only put them down to experience and carry on working with whatever is the best material available.

OUTCROSSING

The term 'outcrossing' is one which is frequently used by breeders. The term is used to define the introduction of a bird into a line or strain of birds to which it bears no direct relationship. Sometimes, it may be found that the birds of a particular line will begin to lose one or more of their good qualities for no apparent reason. When this occurs, breeders employ the use of an **outcross** which is strong in the particular attribute required in order to re-establish it into the line. A common illustration of this is **head size**, and breeders are often heard to remark that they are 'losing their heads'. If a fancier has reached the point at which his birds are breeding true, both genetically and physically but this problem occurs, then, unfortunate though it may be, an outcross must be used. However, very great care must be taken.

It may be all very well to rush out and buy a bird which excells in head size, but if that particular bird carries other *undesirable* points, then the only result will be that these will be bred into the well established line and may well destroy the entire stud, for all practical purposes at least.

At this stage it should be even more apparent that the object of establishing a line of exhibition Budgerigars is not so much breeding in the good points as breeding out bad ones. Having gone to all the trouble to establish a line of birds with a true genotype, therefore, it is not commonsense to breed back into the line a bird which carries bad faults, since the only outcome of this would be to force the breeder to go through the entire process again from the start. Not, I am sure the reader would agree, a desirable state of affairs.

One could go through the process of progeny testing by mating the bird, assuming it to be a cock, with several hens of known genotype and not mating it with the mate for which it was intended until the next breeding season.

By this means, all of the bad points of the outcross will be thrown to the surface, and a decision may then be made on whether it is desirable to introduce it into the true breeding line. The only alternative to this is to take a chance and to mate the bird with its intended mate, and to hope that the progeny from the pairing will carry good points, plus the outstanding point which it is intended to breed back into the line. It is for this reason that the breeder is advised to obtain an outcross from the breeder from which the original stock was obtained, the theory being that such a bird will be very close to the breeders own line, in genetic terms.

Another method of establishing what good or bad points are carried

159

by a particular bird is to mate the same cock with perhaps three different hens during the same breeding season. This is a practice carried out by experienced breeders, and although it is somewhat complicated, it can be achieved with care.

The method is to mate the cock with a hen; then, after mating has been seen to take place, to remove the cock and place him in the breeding cage with the second hen on the evening of the same day. On the following morning he is mated with the third hen, and on that evening, he is reunited with the first hen and so on until all three hens have finished laying.

If this system of breeding is adopted, there are a number of other associated matters to be considered. First, foster parents will be needed, and the fancier will have to be very sure of the ability of the foster pairs to rear their chicks successfully before using them as described. Second, the personality, if one may use the term, of the hens must be taken into consideration. Some hens may not take kindly to their mates being removed in this manner.

In such an event, they may desert the eggs causing them to become chilled and subsequently causing the death of the developing chicks. They may destroy the eggs or indulge in other undesirable behaviour which will have the same effect, and, therefore, one must be very sure of one's stock before undertaking this exercise. I would certainly not advise the breeder to resort to this practice unless the hens have had previous breeding experience, and the same comment applies to the foster parents.

If it can be carried out, however, this method will certainly bring out the bad points inherent in the genotype of the outcross and will provide the breeder with valuable information for future use in the breeding programme.

BROTHER X SISTER

A matter which causes great controversy among Budgerigar breeders is whether one should pair brother to sister. In line breeding, it would appear that this would be a logical pairing in order to reproduce the correct genotype. Unfortunately, however, the constant pairing of brother to sister can and does produce weak offspring and a deterioration, rather than an improvement in the stock. I believe that it is true to say that most serious breeders would not consider this a suitable pairing.

The pairing of half brother to half sister, while not necessarily desirable, is admissible, in that such birds will carry a similar genotype to the pairing of son to mother or daughter to father. Care must be taken, however, and if the birds bred from such pairings should begin to

160

show undesirable traits either from the point of view of visual quality or a falling off in their general health, then the practice should not be continued with that particular line.

DOUBLE FAULTS

From all of this, it should be reasonably apparent that when choosing birds with which a line is being established, under no circumstances should both parents carry the same fault. This point should be especially borne in mind when the original stock is being obtained. As we have seen from the genetic diagrams, breeding two birds together which carry the same fault will simply fix in that bad point and the situation should be avoided completely.

BREEDING AGES

It is usually assumed that the correct age for breeding from the young birds for the first time is ten months for a cock and one year for the hen. Under no circumstances should birds younger than this be used. Using a hen younger than one year old will almost certainly result in egg binding problems, and in all probability problems concerned with the rearing of the chicks. Obviously then, young birds which have been late bred will not be old enough to use in the next breeding season, and this is yet another reason for fanciers prefering to breed as early as possible in the year.

Another factor which must be considered is that it is usually accepted that in the case of a young hen in her first breeding season, one is far better employed in using her with a cock which has already had experience of rearing chicks, especially if the cock has proved himself to be a good father. The young hen will learn by his example, and from such a pairing one has a far greater chance of rearing the chicks to maturity than would be the case if both birds were breeding for the first time.

Theory and Practice

These theories are all very well and appear to be very good on paper, but the beginner should be made aware that there is a vast difference between what one may expect to happen from a particular pairing, and what the result will be in reality. The two are by no means always the same thing! Frequently, a pairing will produce a result quite different from that which is expected, for which there may be no apparent reason, and to which there may be no logical answer. The beginner must be prepared for such disappointments which, it may be said, will certainly occur from time to time.

161

DISPOSING OF LINE BRED STOCK

Another matter of which the beginner should be made aware, is that no young birds should be disposed of until they have gone through their first adult moult. That is, the adult moult as opposed to the nest feather moult. It is by no means unusual for a bird which is considered to be of no particular merit to lose its feathers in the first moult, and to become a bird of very good quality.

A point which the beginner may also like to consider, is that concerning the bird which may have faults, but which carries some outstanding attribute. If, as we have seen, one needs to obtain an outcross for one's line, it is far better to obtain one which already carries a similar genotype. If one retains a bird which perhaps carries good spots or a good head then the bird is instantly available if it is required for breeding back its outstanding points into the line.

This is the reason for some birds being held back by experienced breeders, which, apart from their outstanding point have little else to recommend them, visually at least. It is frequently found that on visiting bird rooms to buy stock, such birds will be seen but will be definitely not for sale. In such cases, the breeder is almost certainly holding the birds back for the purposes already stated. Most experienced breeders adopt this method as a kind of insurance against the day when the line bred stock will begin to lose a good point, and there is no doubt at all that it is a good method of ensuring that one's stud contains a suitable outcross for whatever purpose it may be required.

These then are the methods and reasons behind line breeding. They are based on sound theories which have long been proven in all types of stock breeding, and if consistency is the aim, these are the only methods which will ensure that consistency. To reach the point at which the outcome of a particular pairing from any given line can be predicted accurately will take many breeding seasons, probably many set backs, perhaps even disasters, but when that point is reached, then success is assured.

There is no short cut to success in this respect, and there are three main points to remember. The main one is to begin with good, sound line bred stock of high visual and genetic quality. Take as much advice as is available from experienced breeders, and if in doubt, ask someone who has that experience. Finally, use common sense and never breed a pair of birds together for other than sound genetic reasons.

CHAPTER 10

BREEDING FOR COLOUR

In discussing colour breeding, there are three main factors which must be taken into consideration. First, the sex of the bird, which is important in reproducing what are known as 'sex linked' varieties, second, the colour of the parent bird, and third, the colour which the bird may carry in recessive form in its genotype.

The determination of the sex of the chicks is really quite simple to understand, but its operation serves to illustrate very clearly the manner in which other traits, including colour, are passed on. The male gene is always described diagramatically as **X**, and the female as **Y**. A male has two **X** genes, and a female has one **X** and one **Y** gene. The method by which the sex of the chick is determined is as follows:

With half of the genes from the cock and half of those from the hen coming together (as previously described) in the fertilised ovum, this will give a theoretical expectation as above.

Again, it must be stressed that this is pure theory. If, for example a hen lays five eggs in a clutch, there is nothing to determine whether all five chicks may be cocks or hens. The chances of all five being of one sex are perhaps a little remote, but certainly the possibility exists, which brings us back to the point made earlier, that although the theories are sound, in practice they do not always work out in the manner which we might expect.

The second of our determining factors is that of the colour of the parent bird. We have already seen that green is dominant to all other colours, and the effect this has on the offspring. The third factor is the depth of colour. In the green and blue series, we have light, dark and olive green, and in the blue series, we have sky, cobalt, mauve and violet. The reasons for these variations in colour are the presence or otherwise of what are termed 'dark factors' in the genetic make up of the birds.

Any given bird may have varying combinations of these factors present in its genotype. It may not have them present at all, it may carry one dark factor on one gene and none on the other. It may carry a dark factor on each of its genes, one inherited from its father, the other from its mother.

If we represent the dark factor by a capital letter **D**, and the non-dark factor by the letter **d**, we see that the following combinations can be produced:

This will produce all non-dark factor carrying young.

This will produce 50 per cent single dark factor carrying young, and 50 per cent non-dark factor.

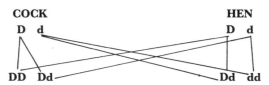

This will produce 25 per cent double dark factor carrying young; 50 per cent single dark factor carrying young, and 25 per cent non-dark factor carrying young.

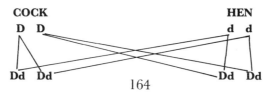

This will produce 100 per cent single dark factor carrying young.

This mating gives 50 per cent double dark factor and 50 per cent single dark factor carrying young.

This pairing will give 100 per cent double dark factor carrying young.

If we now take these pairings and apply them to the green series, taking **g** to represent light green, **G** to represent dark green, and **O** to represent olive green, and substitute these colours for dark and light factor carrying birds, we find:

This pairing gives all light green young.

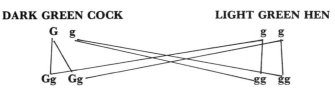

Since the dark factor is dominant to the light, 50 per cent of these young would be dark green and 50 per cent light green.

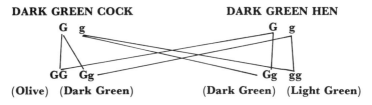

This pairing will give 25 per cent Olive green, 50 per cent dark green and 25 per cent light green.

Thus we have from this pairing 50 per cent olive and 50 per cent dark green.

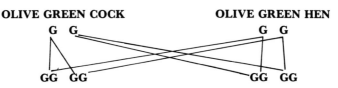

This pairing will give 100 per cent Olive Green.

This pairing of Olive Green to Light Green will give 100 per cent dark green young.

    This formula can be applied in precisely the same manner to the blue series, with the exception of the violet, which has different characteristics and which we will discuss later.

    One point must be very clearly understood, however, before we progress further. The dark factor does not in itself give the bird its colour. It simply has an effect on the depth of that colour. For example: If we mix a gallon of coloured paint with a half gallon of white paint, the resulting colour would be lighter than the original. If we then take two gallons of the coloured paint and mix it with a half gallon of white, the colour would be lighter, but not so light as the first mixture. The dark factor in Budgerigars works in much the same manner.

TYPE I AND TYPE II

    We now have another factor which will have an effect on the colour of the young produced from any given pairing. There are two types of bird, known as Type I and Type II.

    A type I bird is the result of pairing an olive green carrying two dark factors, to a skyblue carrying no dark factors. A type II bird is produced from a mauve, carrying two dark factors, to a light green carrying no dark factor. A point which should be mentioned at this stage is that in discussing birds of one colour which carry a recessive gene for another, as for example green split blue, and written green/blue, the visual colour of the bird is always placed before the oblique, thus, olive green/blue, indicates that the bird is visually olive green, but carries the recessive blue gene.

For practical purposes, more olive greens will be produced from the use of a type I bird and more mauve birds will be produced from the use of a type II. From these matings, however, a very interesting fact emerges. **The results of pairing olive green to skyblue and mauve to light green are visually precisely the same**. How, the reader may well ask, can this be? The reason is really perfectly simple if we remember that green is dominant to all other colours. In the pairing of olive green to skyblue in order to produce type I birds, remember that the olive bird carries two dark genes, which give it the deeper colouration. The skyblue bird carries no dark genes. In this case, the dominant green gene tries to overcome the recessive blue gene, but does not entirely succeed, and results in the double green gene being reduced, at least in effect, and although the resultant offspring are undoubtedly green, they are dark green rather than olive because they carry only one dark factor. They are, of course, split for blue.

In the type II bird, the dominant green factor partly overcomes the recessive double blue gene, and, again, although the bird does become a darker green, it will not have the double green gene to make it an olive green. These birds will also, of course, be split for blue. The use of type I and type II birds is purely in the reproduction of colour. For example: If the breeder wishes to purchase a predominance of mauve birds, or, at least, a relatively large number of this colour, the type II bird should be mated with a mauve; the expectation from this pairing is 50 per cent dark green and 50 per cent mauve. Similarly, if the aim is to produce cobalts, then the pairing is type II to skyblue which will give 50 per cent light green and 50 per cent cobalt.

The type I bird is useful for producing skyblue birds with good even colour, the correct pairing for this purpose being type I to skyblue. Canary breeders have a saying, especially those who specialise in the production of cinnamon varieties. After several generations they 'have a dip into the green', which is usually taken to mean that they are aiming for better colour in their cinnamon varieties. Similar remarks apply to the blue series in budgerigars especially in the skyblue variety, and breeders frequently employ the use of the green varieties after perhaps three or four generations of continual skyblue to skyblue pairing.

The use of type I and type II birds will also produce a small percentage of other colours apart from those already named. For example, a type II bird paired to a mauve, will also give a small percentage of cobalt and olive/blue; the same bird paired with a skyblue will also give small percentages of dark green/blue and skyblue. Similar examples also apply to the type I bird. It is also widely accepted that such minor percentage birds so produced are usually of very good colour, and if a bird of a particular colour is required where colour quality is needed then this is a good method of obtaining such a bird. It should be pointed out, however, that the expectations of the numbers of such birds from any given pairing are so small that one may not breed a single bird of that particular colour.

SEX LINKAGE

In common with other varieties of cage birds, certain types of Budgerigar have a gene for colour linked with their sex cells. These are known as sex linked varieties, and include opaline, cinnamon, slate albino and lutino and the red eyed lacewings. The colour characteristics of these types of birds are passed on in a very specific manner but the important point which should be borne in mind is that the manner of passing on such sex linked inheritance is only through the male side. The superimposition of the sex linked colour is present only on the **X** chromosome, the male factor. We have seen that the cock carries two male chromosomes, while the female carries one **X** and one **Y** chromosome. When the sex cells unite, the offspring will inherit either an **X** chromosome from its mother and an **X** chromosome from its father, in which case it will be a male, or, it may inherit the **X** chromosome from its father and the **Y** chromosome from its mother, in which case it will be a hen.

We have several possible combinations of the opaline factor. In the case of the cock, a bird may carry the factor on both of its sex cells which would make it opaline in appearance and also a true breeding opaline in itself. The cock may have one opaline factor and one normal gene, in which case it would have the normal appearance but would carry the opaline factor hidden in its genotype, or it may have no opaline factor on either chromosome, in which case it would in itself be a true breeding normal. The hen may carry the opaline factor on her **X** chromosome, in which case she will be an opaline, or she may not carry the factor, in which case she will be a normal.

From the foregoing, it can be seen that there can be no such thing as a split opaline normal cock, in the sense that if a cock has a single normal chromosome, it will present a normal appearance, though it may, of course, carry the hidden opaline factor. On the other hand, if the cock is opaline in appearance, then it carries the opaline gene on each of its chromosomes. By the same token, there is no such bird as a split opaline hen. The hen either carries the opaline factor on her **X** gene, in which case she will be opaline in appearance, or she does not, in which case she will be a normal.

We can now look at the outcome of the variations of the possible opaline factor carrying birds in diagramatic form, taking capital **X** to represent the opaline factor, and **x** to represent the normal or non–opaline factor.

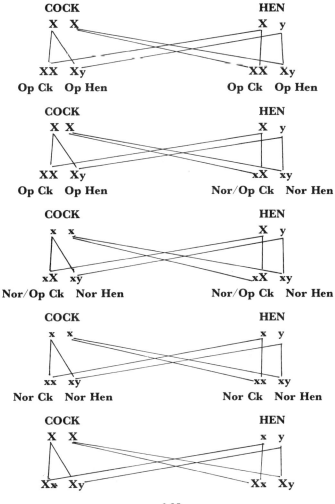

COCK   HEN
X X   X y
XX Xy   XX Xy
Op Ck Op Hen   Op Ck Op Hen

COCK   HEN
X X   X y
XX Xy   xX xy
Op Ck Op Hen   Nor/Op Ck Nor Hen

COCK   HEN
x x   X y
xX xy   xX xy
Nor/Op Ck Nor Hen   Nor/Op Ck Nor Hen

COCK   HEN
x x   x y
xx xy   xx xy
Nor Ck Nor Hen   Nor Ck Nor Hen

COCK   HEN
X X   x y
Xx Xy   Xx Xy

To work out the expectancy from any of the sex linked varieties, simply substitite the particular variety for the opaline factor on the above series of diagrams.

Having discussed the factors which give the birds their colour, we must now consider which pairings are best for the production of good solid coloured birds. The main point to consider when colour production is the aim, is that the green series birds are basically birds with a yellow ground, with the colour 'superimposed', for want of a better expression, upon it, whereas the blue series of birds are basically white ground birds, again with the colour superimposed.

It is the background colour of the birds which gives the albino and lutino their colours. Both are albinos, in that the substance which gives the birds their colouring — melanin — the same substance which in humans gives the colour of the hair and eyes, is absent, leaving the birds in as it were their natural state. It should also be noted that both albino and lutino have the characteristic red eyes of the albino.

Light Green

In many cases, it is found that in the intermediate colours, dark green, cobalt and so on, a pairing of the lighter colour with that of the double factor dark will produce intermediate colours with a better overall colour than if those intermediate colours were interbred. In the case of the light green, however, this is not so, and the best method of producing this colour to a desirable degree is to mate only light green to light green, but to ensure that the birds being used are of good colour.

Dark Green

There are two methods of producing 100 per cent dark greens and, at the same time, the type I and type II birds which we discussed earlier. Either by crossing a mauve with a light green (type II) or an olive green with a skyblue, type I. The pairing of olive green to light green will also give 100 per cent dark green, and with one colour balancing the other, this is probably a good method of producing good dark greens.

Olive Green

The best pairing for producing olive greens of good deep colour is simply olive to olive.

Skyblue

To produce 100 per cent skyblues, as in the green series, the correct pairing is skyblue to skyblue. Excellent skyblues have been produced from the crossing of skyblue and cobalt, and it should also be remembered that the introduction of green bloodlines into the skyblue line should be carried out after perhaps three or at most four generations.

170

If a light green/blue bird is used in this pairing, then more blue birds will be produced, and these will almost certainly improve the colour of the blue line.

Cobalt

The rules relating to the production of dark greens can also be applied to the cobalt. If a mauve is paired to a skyblue, then the resulting cobalts will probably be of good colour, and this pairing will produce 100 per cent cobalt.

Mauve

If the breeder wishes to breed mauves in quantity, then the obvious pairing is mauve to mauve, both birds carrying a double dark factor; the result of which will be 100 per cent mauve offspring. It is usually accepted, however, that the best pairing from which rich coloured mauves can be produced, while at the same time retaining a good type, is that of olive/blue to mauve. Such a pairing would produce 50 per cent olive/blue and 50 per cent mauve.

Violet

The violet has a number of rules governing its production which must be clearly understood before any attempt is made to breed this variety. The first is that the violet character is dominant, and, therefore, no bird can be split for violet. It is either violet, or it is not. The second point is that since the character is dominant, it can be bred into every colour, giving violet mauve, violet sky blue, violet light green, violet olive and so on. Thirdly, the only bird which has the completely visual violet appearance is the violet cobalt. Other birds which are described, for example, as being violet sky blue, are sky blue birds which show the darker violet character in their colouring, but they are certainly not visually the deep violet colour of the violet cobalt, the true violet. Similarly with all the other varieties; a violet mauve, for example is a mauve bird which has the violet present in its phenotype but, again, it is not violet in the true sense of the word.

Lastly, to be a true violet, that is, a cobalt violet, a bird must be bred from the blue series, it must carry one dark factor, and a single or double factor for violet.

BREEDING COMBINATIONS AND EXPECTATIONS

There are sixteen possible combinations in the violet series, all of which will produce offspring carrying the violet character in greater or lesser percentages. Not all of them will produce the true violet bird, the violet cobalt, and there are exceptions to the normal rules which will become apparent in the following diagrams.

Before going further, the reader should realise that prior to working out the percentages expected from any given pairing, we must know how the parent birds were bred. For example, a violet mauve would be the result of pairing violet mauve to violet mauve, whereas a violet sky blue would be bred from violet sky blue to violet or sky blue. Therefore, a single factor mauve bird would have violet mauve on one gene and mauve on the other, and a double factor mauve would have a violet factor on each of its genes. A single factor violet is represented as **Vm** for the violet character and **m** for the mauve. In the case of the violet cobalt the dark character, as opposed to the violet character, is represented by the capital **C** and the light character by **c**, thus, we have all the possible combinations of light and dark characters. Having established that, we can now begin to calculate the expectations. The pairing of a single factor violet sky blue VS s to a mauve M M would give:

In this pairing, the conjunction of the gene for violet sky blue with the double dark factor **M** would produce a cobalt bird in the same way as the simple sky blue to mauve pairing, the violet factor present on the **VS** gene, would, however, since it is dominant, produce a violet cobalt. The conjunction of the normal **s** gene from the violet sky blue with the two mauve genes would produce exactly the same result as pairing sky blue to mauve, i.e. a cobalt bird carrying one dark factor from the mauve and the other light factor from the sky blue. The following diagrams can be worked out in exactly the same manner.

Double Factor Violet Sky Blue to Mauve

For the production of violets (violet cobalt), this is clearly the best pairing since it produces 100 per cent visual violet.

Single Factor Sky Blue to Cobalt
(**C** for dark factor inherited from parents and **s** for light factor)

If a cobalt and sky blue are crossed the result is 50 per cent sky blue and 50 per cent cobalt, because:

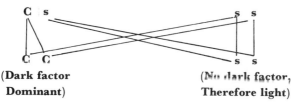

(**Dark factor**   (**No dark factor,**
Dominant)   **Therefore light**)

Double Factor Sky Blue to Cobalt

Single Factor Sky Blue to Sky Blue

Double Factor Sky Blue to Sky Blue

Single Factor Cobalt to Sky Blue

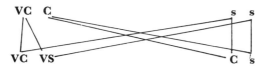

Double Factor Cobalt to Sky Blue

SINGLE FACTOR COBALT TO COBALT

If we continue with the diagrams as drawn above, it would appear that the logical outcome of this pairing would be 50 per cent violet cobalt, 25 per cent sky blue and 25 per cent cobalt. Remembering, however, what was said concerning the factors inherited from the parents, we see that these birds have a more complex inheritance as follows.

Our violet cobalt would be the result of pairing violet mauve with sky blue cobalt on the one hand, and mauve with sky blue on the other. The normal cobalt would be the result of mauve to sky blue and mauve to sky blue. For reasons of clarity, we must now alter the diagram a little. We now have two birds which carry in their genotypes

1	2	3	4	5	6	7	8
VM	s	M	s	M	s	M	s

If we take the violet mauve gene from the cock and add this to each of the genes from the hen on the right, we have the following combinations:

VM M = VM; VM s = VC; VM M = VM and VM s = VC

Taking this to its logical conclusion and pairing gene 1 with genes 5, 6, 7, 8; gene 2 with genes 5, 6, 7, 8 and so on, we find, the following, reading each combination from top to bottom:

1:5,6,7,8.	2:5,6,7,8.	3:5,6,7,8.	4:5,6,7,8.
VM	VC	M	C
VC	VS	C	S
VM	VC	M	C
VC	VS	C	S

This, if the table is examined will give the Mendelian 1:2:1 pattern in both violet and dark factor carrying birds and in the non carrying birds. The result of all this, is that $12\frac{1}{2}$ per cent violet sky blue, 25 per cent violet cobalt, $12\frac{1}{2}$ per cent violet mauve, $12\frac{1}{2}$ per cent sky blue, 25 per cent cobalt and $12\frac{1}{2}$ per cent mauve birds will be produced. Theoretically at least, there are two violet mauves, four violet cobalts, two violet sky blue, two mauve, four cobalt and two skyblue, again, the 1:2:1 pattern.

It must be stressed very strongly at this point, that these expectations are only theoretical outcomes of the various pairings: if you like, possibilities. We must now revert to what was said on the subject of the formation of the sex cells.

During fertilisation of the ovum, many hundreds of sex cells are involved, and remembering that which sex cell from the cock meets which sex cell from the hen is purely a matter of chance, the reader will no doubt gather that the expected outcome of any pairing is vague, to say the least. For example, no one is able to state with certainty that in the example of violet cobalt to cobalt, two sky blue offspring will be produced. The nearest one is able to come is to say that working on an average of a number of pairings, the percentages would very probably work out as set down here.

VIOLET COBALT TO VIOLET COBALT

It would appear, on the surface, that the best method of producing visual violets, would be to pair violet cobalt to violet cobalt, but for reasons which are explained in the diagram below, that is not so. We must again take into consideration the genetic colour factors in the birds, and we have

1	2	3	4	5	6	7	8
VM	S	M	S	VM	S	M	S

If we now carry out the same exercise as that in the previous diagram, we have:

1:5,6,7,8.	2:5,6,7,8.	3:5,6,7,8.	4:5,6,7,8.
VM	VC	VM	VC
VC	VS	VC	VS
VM	VC	M	C
VC	VS	C	S

The theoretical expectations are therefore, three violet mauve, six violet cobalt, three violet sky blue, one sky blue, two cobalt and one mauve, corresponding to approximate percentages of 20, 40, 20, 5, 10 and 5.

Having explained the above two matings, we can now return to our previous diagrams.

Double Factor Cobalt to Cobalt

Single Factor Mauve to Skyblue

Double Factor Mauve to Sky Blue

Single Factor Mauve to Cobalt

Double Factor Mauve to Cobalt

Single Factor Mauve to Mauve

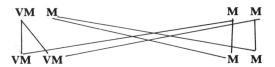

Double Factor Mauve to Mauve

This, then, is the manner in which the violet factor is passed on. As we have seen, it can, because of its dominent nature, be passed to any colour, and in some, for example, olive green or clearwing types, it can and does help to evolve extremely attractive birds. Similar remarks apply to the violet concerning the introduction of green blood into the line as apply to the non–violet bird, in that the introduction of green blood after several generations will deepen the colour and help to keep it even, which is an essential feature.

GREY

There are three types of grey Budgerigars. The Australian Dominant Grey, which has two distinct forms, the single and double factor grey, and the English Grey which is a recessive type. If, however a grey appears on the show bench, it is almost 100 per cent certain that it is an Australian Grey, since the English type is almost non-existent.

Like the violet the Australian Grey is dominant, and there can be no such bird as a split grey, the bird is either grey or it is not. Equally, the grey factor can be introduced visually into all of the varieties, producing olive green, grey green, and so on. Also in the violet series, the double factor grey cross light grey produces single factor (mid grey) birds of good colour. A particular favourite with producers of grey birds is the grey green/blue with medium grey, which produces birds of good type and excellent colour. For colour expectations from the grey series, the reader should study the diagrams concerned with violet inheritance and substitute the grey factor for the violet. The results will be precisely the same.

LUTINO

There are two types of Lutino, a bird which, as we have already noted, is solely the ground colour of the green variety. The main one, for our purposes, is the sex linked variety. The genetic inheritance of the lutino is precisely the same as that for cinnamon, and any conclusions to be made on this point can be worked out using the diagram concerning opaline inheritance. Because of the sex linkage, the same rules apply, in that a lutino hen will have the lutino factor present on her **X** gene, in which case she will be lutino, and since this factor cannot be present on her **Y** gene, the female determining gene, she cannot pass on the lutino factor to her daughters, but only to her sons through the **X** gene. If the lutino factor is not present on her **X** gene, then the hen will be a normal, and like the other sex linked varieties, it is impossible for a hen to be split for a sex linked variety.

177

A cock, however, which has the two **X** genes, may, if it has been produced by pairing a normal cock to a lutino hen, be normal in appearance, but will carry the lutino carrying **X** gene from the hen, its mother. The best method of producing lutinos from a colour standpoint is to pair lutino to lutino, which would give 100 per cent lutino offspring, but as in the case of the blue series, after several generations, the type of the birds may begin to degenerate, at which point the usual practice is to introduce green back into the line, using a normal cock to a lutino hen, which will result in normal cocks split for lutino, and lutino hens. The trouble, so far as the lutino colouring is concerned, with such a combination, is that the green colour of the normal bird will manifest itself visually in the young, and will have to be bred out again by using the split lutino cocks and lutino hens.

If such a bird is obtainable, the best one to use for the purpose of reintroducing type in lutinos is a good light yellow, but such birds are not easily acquired, or, for that matter, easily found.

ALBINO

The albino, which is pure white in colour, is the ground colour from the blue series, and exactly the same rules apply to this type as to the lutino, except that if a normal split albino is being used for any reason with the albino strain, then the normal should be of the blue series.

LUTINO/ALBINO

It is possible, by introducing the green/blue bird into the lutino strain, to produce young which would have the genetic make up required to produce both lutino and albino young, depending upon whether they are mated to the green series or the blue series. Whether there is any practical advantage from the deliberate use of such pairings is very much a matter for debate, especially since there are much easier methods of producing lutinos than by going through the somewhat complicated process.

NON-SEX LINKED LUTINOS

There is another type of lutino, which, like the English Grey, is virtually non-existent. This is the non-sex linked lutino. The production of lutinos from this type of bird is far more of a hit and miss affair than it is when the sex linked types are used. For that reason, few breeders deliberately breed this type of lutino, largely because the mating of such a bird with a sex-linked type would result in young, the breeding characteristics of which would be impossible to predict with any degree of accuracy.

YELLOW

The main difference between true yellow and the lutino, is that the yellow colour of the lutino is caused by the absence of melanin, whereas the colour of the yellow is a colour as such. There is also a difference in the eyes; the yellow, being a normal bird has the black eyes characterising the normal while the lutino has the red eyes of the albino. The breeding of yellows follows the normal breeding rules, and the bird is not sex linked. If good yellows can be found, there may be a case for breeding such birds with the lutinos, and thereby serving the double purpose of lightening the yellow colour in the yellow offspring, and also, as we have already noted, improving the type of a strain of lutinos which may be dropping in quality.

PIED VARIETIES

There are three main types of pied variety, namely, the Dominant Pied, the pied which has roughly the top part of the body in the colours of the colour series of the bird from which it was bred, and ending just above the thighs in a straight line around the body. The bottom half of the bird is in the ground colour of the colour series, so that in a Dominant Pied bred from the green series the bird would be green and yellow, or in the blue series, blue and white.

There is the dominant banded pied, the bird which has a clearly distinguished band of colour around its body, and usually referred to as the Australian Banded Pied, after the country of its origin. The third type is the recessive pied, which has patches of colour throughout, and because of its recessive nature, this type has quite different genetic rules than those of the dominant varieties. Since both dominant varieties have the same pattern of genetic inheritance, we are able to take the two together, and the outcome of any pairing, whether it be straightforward dominant pied or banded pied, is the same. It should be noted that pied varieties may also carry dark or light factors, and can be produced in any colour, the dark factor working in the same manner as it does in the normal varieties. If, for example, an olive green pied is mated to a light green pied, the resulting chicks will be single dark factor carrying dark green, but will of course be pied.

If we now apply these formulae of genetic inheritance in diagrammatic form, taking **P** for the pied factor and **n** for the normal, we have:

179

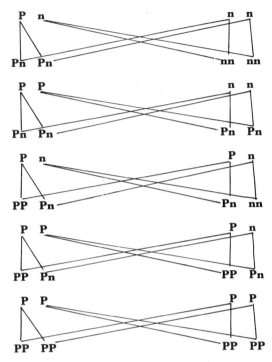

Where the genetic constitution is made up of, for example, **Pn**, the bird will be visually pied because of the dominance of the pied factor.

From the above diagrams, it appears that the best method of producing pied varieties is to mate double factor pied with double factor pied. If the object is to produce pied birds, with other considerations, as for example type, being unimportant, then such is the case. If, however, one wishes to produce pied with good size, type, heads and so on, then it is generally accepted among breeders that the pied varieties should be crossed with the normal varieties. The recessive character of the other variety of pied bird, the recessive pied, is quite different from that of the dominant pied. Referring to the diagrams of the dominant pied inheritance, however, we can substitute **r** for **P** to indicate the recessive gene, and capital **N** to indicate the dominance of the normal gene over the recessive, and we have:

and so on.

The difference in the birds produced, however, is that whereas those from the dominant types and carrying the dominant pied gene will be visually pied, those produced from the recessive pairings will only be visually pied if they carry the double recessive gene, one from each parent.

The best method of producing recessive pieds, which are unquestionably a very pleasing bird from a purely aesthetic standpoint, is to pair a double recessive carrying pied, i.e. a visual pied, to another similar bird. The next best method would be to pair a double recessive, i.e. a pied, with a normal/pied, which would produce half visual pied and half normal/pied.

On the subject of distinguishing between the different varieties of pieds, I would refer the reader to the colour standards, and especially to those points concerning the colour of the eyes. For example, the eye of the dominant pied is black with a white iris ring as in the normal varieties, the recessive pied has a solid dark eye.

YELLOW, WHITE AND GREYWING VARIETIES

These varieties constitute what is termed the clearwing group, but since the greywing varieties are met with very infrequently, it is probably unimportant to enter too far into their inheritance patterns, which are quite complicated, in that using the bird in the normal manner can result in some rather indeterminate results. If the breeder is interested in colour production for its own sake, however, then the introduction of greywing varieties along with whitewing or yellow wing factors and perhaps adding dark factors, can result in some interesting colours. Whether such birds would be of sufficient quality to be successful on the show bench is, however, another matter entirely. I believe it is true to say that few, if any breeders use the greywing varieties from which to produce birds of exhibition standard. For our purposes, the yellow wing and whitewing birds are the important ones from an exhibition point of view.

If the reader wishes to introduce such birds into his stud in order to produce birds for the show bench, then all he needs to do, is to remember that the factor for either yellow wing or whitewing, is recessive to the normal green or blue. If we refer back to the genetic inheritance patterns of the recessive pied, and substitute yellow wing or whitewing, depending upon whether the bird is bred from the green or blue series, the outcome of any given pairing is the same as that of the recessive pied. There is a curious cross over effect with clearwings when they are paired to normal yellows or whites, in that the factor then becomes dominant. Since, however, the aim is to produce yellow winged or whitewinged birds, a bird produced from, for example, a whitewing blue and a white, will be completely white in any event, the question is surely academic, though it may be argued that such pairings may produce even clearer wings than those of the clearwing to clearwing pairing. As with, for example, the pied varieties, the clearwing factor can be produced in all shades of colour.

YELLOW FACED FACTOR

The yellow faced factor is usually applied to the blue series, since, in the logical manner, the factor is linked to the green series, yellow being the ground colour of this series, and as we have already noted, dominant to all other colours. A yellow faced green would therefore simply have the appearance of a normal green. Because of its green inheritance, the yellow face factor becomes dominant when it is introduced in the blue series, and therefore, the result of pairing a yellow face factor carrying bird with, for example a sky blue, would be half yellow face and half normal blue. Again, the formula can be applied to the diagram showing pied inheritance, the yellow face factor being substituted for the pied factor **P**.

As with other varieties, yellow faced characteristics can be introduced into all of the other existing varieties, including the pied varieties, giving almost unlimited combinations of colour. Probably the most popular is the so called rainbow, which is in fact a combination of opaline clearwing and yellow faced, these characteristics being combined with the blue series. The correct term for a rainbow is an opaline clearwing yellow faced blue.

FALLOW

There is a variety of Budgerigar known as the fallow. This type has brown as opposed to cinnamon markings in place of the normal black barring. Like the Australian Banded Pied, this variety is often referred to as the German Fallow for the same reason, i.e. it originated in Germany.

There is an English variety in existence, but like the pied varieties, the types can be distinguished from the colour of the eyes.

The diagramatic inheritance patterns of the fallow are; where **F** represents Fallow and **N**, normal:

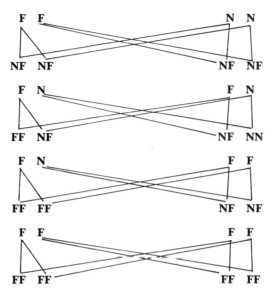

The fallow factor is, therefore, recessive to normal, and any birds which carry only one factor for fallow, will be visually normal. Only those birds which carry the double fallow factor will be visual fallows.

GENERAL REMARKS

From all of the above, the reader will no doubt have gathered that in most cases, there is some method or other of introducing most of the factors described into the various colour forms. It should also be clear that these can be introduced in multiple form, as for example the rainbow referred to earlier, or for example opaline cinnamon greywing or whatever. This only serves to underline the importance of keeping breeding records because unless the colour inheritance of the parent bird is known, then there is no possible chance of predicting the outcome of any given pairing no matter what the colour involved.

Several times in this chapter, I have mentioned that the colour expectations are theoretical, and can in no way be taken to be precise. This point must be stressed, especially when the earlier remarks concerning the chance coincidence of the colour carrying, and for that matter, other genes are taken into consideration. It may well be that, for example, a pairing of two single factor birds, which would, in theory, be expected to produce 25 per cent, 50 per cent and 25 per cent colour expectations, may in practice produce 100 per cent of one particular variety, though it should be stated that this is unlikely. Whether or not the pairing would produce one, two and one chicks from any given four, is, in my view equally unlikely. From the examples given, and assuming a large number of pairings were made with the same genetic ingredients, the probability in terms of numbers of the variously coloured young produced is as set down.

In order to work out the likely expectations from any combination, the breeder must be aware of the genetic make up of the bird in terms of the colour inherited from the parents. Whether the bird in question carries none, one or two of the factors involved, and whether the factor is dominant or recessive.

When these factors are known, and are related to the diagrams in this chapter, the outcome of any pairing can be ascertained, at least in theory, and will almost certainly produce some of the desired colour varieties for which the breeder is aiming.

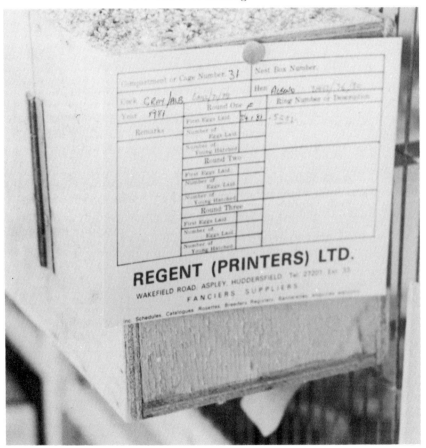

Figure 10.1 A comprehensive record is essential if one is breeding for colour

CHAPTER 11

DISEASES, PARASITES AND
HEALTH CARE

AIM FOR PREVENTION

The best method of dealing with diseases and ailments in the bird room is their prevention in the first instance. There are a number of sources which will cause disease of one type or another, and before examining the specific diseases affecting Budgerigars, the reader should be made aware of the major sources of this type of trouble. A draughty or damp bird room will cause respiratory troubles; probably in the first instance, colds, which will in turn lead to more serious disorders if the birds are not treated immediately. Dirty food containers will cause diseases of the alimentary canal, the digestive system, as will stale food, especially stale egg food. Another common cause of a number of birds becoming ill with the same disease, is that of leaving an affected bird in a flight with other birds. For example, scaly-face will very rapidly affect other stock if an infected bird is allowed to come into contact. Regardless of whether the disease in question is considered to be communicable or not, it is essential that any bird suffering from any disease should be isolated immediately upon discovery.

The main factor to be considered in the treatment of all diseases of Budgerigars is that treatment should be immediate. For example, a simple case of diarrhoea, if treated immediately, will almost certainly clear up, but if it is left untreated, it may well develop into enteritis or even typhoid, in which case the breeder has a far greater and far more serious problem on his hands. Diseases in Budgerigars develop extremely quickly, and birds affected with certain diseases will die equally quickly if treatment is not immediate. When a disease has taken a firm hold on a particular bird, the chances of its recovery are not very

185

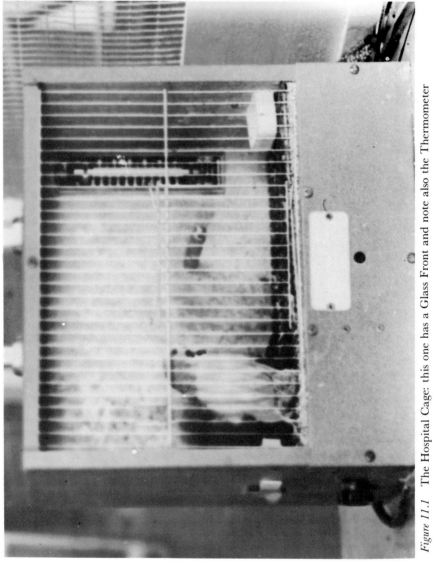

Figure 11.1   The Hospital Cage: this one has a Glass Front and note also the Thermometer

high, and in certain diseases, treatment of the entire bird room may be necessary, indeed, essential, as, for example following the onset of Avian Tuberculosis. Disease in breeding rooms is by no means so common as may be supposed, but if it should occur, then it cannot be stressed sufficiently strongly that treatment must be immediate. It is for these reasons that the advice concerning the thorough cleaning of the entire bird room is given in the chapter on general management and that this must be carried out at least twice each year, preferably before and after the breeding season.

The three main causes of disease are dirt in the bird room, draughts and damp, and dirty, dusty seed. If these three major causes can be eliminated, which, by judicious and careful management they surely can, then any breeder who experiences diseases among his stock may count himself unfortunate.

GENERAL SIGNS OF DISEASE

The general signs of disease in Budgerigars are frequently referred to by fanciers as symptoms, quite incorrectly, since there is no such thing as a symptom in Budgerigars. A symptom is a part of the disease which a patient is able to tell his doctor, as for example headache or abdominal pains. Since a Budgerigar cannot tell the breeder of such matters, the breeder will have to proceed upon the basis of treating those signs which he can see. Because of this, the breeder must use his eyes when carrying out the daily routine of caring for his stock, and should make it a part of that routine to look for signs of disease.

The main points so far as the stock is concerned, are a general listlessness in the behaviour of the bird; a bird which sits dejectedly on its perch, perhaps with its feathers fluffed out, and more especially so if the tail is rising and falling rhythmically with what is usually termed a pumping action. A bird in such a condition is almost certainly in pain and should be attended to immediately on humanitarian grounds alone, quite apart from the value of the bird to the breeder. The droppings of the birds should be examined, and if there is any sign of their being loose, and more especially if they appear to be more green than normal, action must be taken. The area around the beak and the eyes should merit a check, because a discharge from the eyes may indicate a more serious condition. Similarly with the beak. A bird which has perhaps been vomiting will have some signs of that fact on its chest or under the beak. The cere should be examined for signs of scaly face, as also should the feet and legs for signs of a similar disease. If an alimentary disorder is suspected, then the vent area should be inspected. In such diseases, a sign common to all is loose droppings, varying

187

according to the specific diseases. For example, in enteritis, the droppings will have a green and slimy appearance which will stain the vent green.

Obviously one cannot examine each bird minutely every day, but some system of quickly looking the birds over during the feeding process may well pay dividends in the early discovery and treatment of a disease, and, what is perhaps more important, will prevent its spread to other stock. In any event, a good idea is to have a twice weekly medical check and to observe each bird individually for a few moments, taking in the points mentioned. Such a procedure may save a valuable bird or birds.

DISEASES OF THE RESPIRATORY SYSTEM

The respiratory system consists basically of the mouth and nose, the trachea, which leads from the throat to the top of the lungs, the bronchial tubes which divide at that point, one part going into each tube. These then lead directly into the lung and are again divided and sub-divided until they reach the bottom of the lung. The lungs are sponge-like masses containing hundreds of small air sacs called alveoli, their purpose being to distribute air to the bloodstream.

Scaly-Face

Scaly-face is not strictly a disease, but a condition caused by a tiny mite, which produces white, apparently fungoid, growth around the cere and nostrils. Its effect is upon the respiratory system, and it is, therefore, included in this section. If the condition is allowed to go untreated, it will eventually grow over the nostrils and will cause distress to the bird. The cause of scaly-face is dirty perches, and it is usually contracted by the birds scraping their beaks in accumulated dirt. It is highly contagious, and is passed on because of the habit which Budgerigars have of tapping their beaks together. Treatment is very simple and very effective; even the most extensive cases can be cleared up quite quickly. A twice daily application of Benzyl Benzoate applied with a small brush will clear up the problem, and there are proprietary preparations available at pet stores which will also clear up the condition quickly.

Scaly Legs

Although it is not a respiratory disease, scaly legs is also included here, because the mite which causes scaly face also causes this particular problem. The cause is the same, as is the treatment, and a bird suffering from scaly legs will have the white nodules on the legs rather than the face. Both conditions should be treated immediately because of their rapid spread among the stock.

The way to prevent scaly-face and scaly legs is to make sure that all of the perches in the stock cages and flights are kept clean at all times, and that the cages and flights in general are kept clean.

Thrush

Thrush is a fungoid growth which attacks the mouth, and which is distinguished by a greyish membrane covering the inside of the mouth and the throat. If the membrane is removed, small ulcers may be seen beneath which have the appearance of small white spots. The cause of this disease is dirt in the cages and feeding utensils especially. Treatment is the provision of a small amount of permanganate of potash, using just sufficient to colour the drinking water. One sign of the onset of thrush is that the bird will refuse its food, but will show no obvious signs of any other disease which would cause it to do so.

Bronchitis

This disease affects the bronchial tubes, causing inflammation. The affected bird will probably have pains in the chest area, and its breathing will be laboured and audible. It may also sit on its perch with its beak open gasping for air. The faeces may be loose and yellowish in appearance, although this does not always follow.

The treatment of bronchitis is to remove the bird from the flight or stock cage to some place of warmth, making sure that it is draught proof, and to treat the condition with antibiotics, possibly aureomycin, administered on the advice of a veterinary surgeon.

Asthma

The signs of asthma affecting a bird are very similar to those of bronchitis. The problem so far as asthma is concerned, is that there may well be a recurrence. The breeder will have to consider whether a bird which continues to have recurring troubles of this nature should be kept, since it will almost certainly be useless for either breeding or showing purposes. The treatment is the same as that for bronchitis, but the prognosis is not so good. Both conditions are caused by draught or damp surroundings.

Colds

Budgerigars like other forms of animal life can contract colds, especially in draughty surroundings. The importance of treating a bird with a cold is that an untreated cold may very quickly develop into something more serious. A cold may turn rapidly to pneumonia, in which case the bird will certainly die unless treatment is extremely quick, and it may do so in any event. It may be useful to stress here that such diseases as pneumonia are extremely dangerous in Budgerigars,

189

and tend to be fatal within perhaps only two days.

The way to prevent colds is simply to make sure that the birds have an even temperature in the bird room and are not subjected to extremes of cold and heat, especially during the winter months.

Pneumonia

The signs of pneumonia are rapid breathing, a discharge from the nostrils, sneezing, and the bird gasping for breath. The bird will also have pain in the chest, and the specific signs will be accompanied by the general signs of illness discussed earlier. Treatment is removal of the bird, preferably to a hospital cage where it can be kept warm, but certainly to isolation and treatment with antibiotics, which, again, should be given in line with veterinary advice.

Avian Tuberculosis

Avian Tuberculosis is a rare disease among Budgerigars, but it may occur. It is caused by a bacillus, a rod like organism, and practical treatment is almost impossible. The signs of this disease are a rapid loss of weight, coupled with diarrhoea or even dysentery. The birds affected by this wasting disease will almost certainly die, even if they are treated, and in any event will be no further use for breeding or showing purposes, even if they are cured. The only humane treatment for a bird suffering in this manner is to have it painlessly destroyed.

The problem then, however, is that the entire bird room must be extremely thoroughly disinfected. Every corner must be thoroughly scrubbed with disinfectant, and an important factor is that the doors and windows must be left open as much as possible in order to allow as much direct sunlight into the room as is practicable. The organisms which cause tuberculosis live in the dust, but they cannot survive in direct sunlight. The breeder must, therefore, eliminate the dust entirely, no matter how long it takes, and then admit the sunlight. The reader should also be made aware that the tubercule bacillus can survive for great lengths of time, lying dormant in dust and awaiting the opportunity to attack living tissue.

Aspergillosis

Aspergillosis is a fungoid disease which attacks the lung tissue. Like all such diseases, the organism which causes the disease is spore borne. A bird so infected will cough out the spores which will then be airborne in the bird room and will eventually be breathed in by the remaining stock. It is an extremely dangerous disease in any bird room for that reason.

Apart from the general signs of illness, the bird will lose weight extremely rapidly and will have difficulty in breathing. The distinguishing feature of aspergillosis is that the bird will have a tendency to drink far more than normal. As with avian tuberculosis, treatment is impracticable, and a bird suffering from this disease should be destroyed. If such a bird is found in the aviary, however, the breeder may count himself very fortunate indeed if only one case is discovered. The cause is dirt in the bird room, and this is very much a case of prevention being better than cure. If it should occur, the entire bird room should be stripped down and cleaned as thoroughly as possible with strong disinfectant. At the same time, a very close watch should be kept on the remaining stock in an attempt to remove any other birds which may be affected at the first signs of the disease.

Psittacosis

Psittacosis is probably the best known of all diseases affecting Budgerigars, especially so since it is transmittable to humans. Fortunately, the incidence of this disease is very much smaller than some appear to believe, and it is, in fact, a rather rare disease. Unfortunately, the signs of psittacosis are very similar indeed to those of pneumonia, but it has a distinctly sinister side to it, in that it is caused by a virus which, like the tubercule bacillus, can lie dormant for several months. Treatment is impracticable, and because the signs are so similar to those of pneumonia, it can only be diagnosed with certainty by post mortem examination.

The sign which would make one suspicious of this disease in a breeding room, is that a stud of birds begins to contract what appears to be pneumonia one after the other. Since the treatment for pneumonia is to isolate the bird and apply warmth and antibiotics, it is doubtful whether this disease is transmittable in the accepted sense of the word. Psittacosis is, however, a different matter, and the virus can be spread around the bird room by the affected bird. Assuming that the bird room is free of damp and draughts, then where there appears to be an unusual incidence of apparent pneumonia, it is best to make sure whether disease is in fact pneumonia or psittacosis, by laboratory examination.

DISEASES OF THE ALIMENTARY CANAL

Many of the diseases affecting the alimentary canal — the digestive system — show similar signs. In quite a large number of such cases, the differences between the various diseases, as for example enteritis and infestation of the birds by organisms called **E.Coli**, are purely academic, since the treatment may be the same.

The reader should also be made aware that in many cases, the treatment of birds with antibiotics can be very much a hit and miss affair. There are, for example, many types of **E.Coli** or **Salmonella**, (the organism which causes food poisoning in humans); some will react to one type of antibiotic while remaining strong and unaffected by another. In the treatment of cage birds, and especially those diseases affecting the digestive system, therefore, the outcome of treatment is something of an unknown quantity. If, by chance, the organism causing the specific disease is immune to the particular antibiotic being administered, by the time the breeder discovers this unfortunate fact, the bird is probably dead.

It is in such cases that laboratory post mortems are of value; if the specific organism is isolated, the veterinary surgeon is able to supply the precise treatment against that particular organism and if there is a recurrence in the bird room, the other birds affected may be saved.

Enteritis

Enteritis is by far the most common disease of the digestive system found in bird rooms. The cause is draughts or dampness which cause chills and subsequent inflammation of the bowel. There are two main types of enteritis, gastro-enteritis, which is inflammation of the stomach and bowel, and enteritis, which is inflammation of the bowel only. Since the treatment of both conditions is the same, the differences are unimportant.

A bird suffering from enteritis will have the typical fluffed appearance of a sick bird. The main sign is that the droppings will be green and slimy and the vent will be stained green. The bird should be isolated and kept warm, warmth being of especial importance, and antibiotics given on veterinary advice.

If treatment is begun immediately, there is no reason at all why the bird should not recover completely. Usually, this happens very quickly but care should be taken when returning the bird from its warm surroundings to the lower temperature of the bird room. If the bird does recover quickly, which may be within 24 hours, treatment should be continued for at least another two days to make sure that there is no recurrence.

E.Coli

A term often used incorrectly by fanciers to describe a particular type of disease of the digestive tract is **E.Coli**. This is not in itself a disease, but is the general name under which a group of bacteria called **Escherichia Coli** are labelled. The reason for this is that there are a number of organisms which all cause the same signs, but unfortunately for Budgerigar breeders, they do not all react to the same treatment.

Again, a bird suffering from a disease caused by one of these organisms will display the usual symptoms of listlessness, loss of appetite and will be hunched on the perch with its feathers fluffed out. The main sign is a yellow coloured diarrhoea. This is strictly a case of hit and miss so far as treatment is concerned. Veterinary advice must be sought immediately, and the breeder will only be able to hope that a broad spectrum antibiotic will, as it were, hit the target with the first shot. If it does, then so well and good. If it does not, then the bird must be subjected to post mortem examination so that the veterinary surgeon will know which specific antibiotic will be effective.

As in the treatment of most diseases of Budgerigars a bird so affected must be isolated and placed in a warm environment.

Salmonella

Another disease which attacks Budgerigars is the organism which causes food poisoning in humans, and known as salmonella, *Salmonella Typhosus* otherwise known as typhoid.

The habit which Budgerigars have of eating the droppings of other birds is the method by which infection is spread, and it is possible for a bird to carry this disease without itself displaying any of the signs or suffering itself. The specific disease is difficult to detect without laboratory examination; the only real outward sign, apart from the normal signs of general illness, is that there may be diarrhoea, possibly predominantly white in appearance. Treatment is by antibiotics, again, on veterinary advice.

Diarrhoea

Diarrhoea in its simplest form is not dangerous and can be cleared up very quickly. Possible causes are dirty feeding utensils and stale food, or dirt in the cages. In a case of simple diarrhoea, the bird may not exhibit general signs of illness, but may simply have loose droppings. Treatment is the placing of two drops of Kaolin mixture in two fluid ounces of water, which should quickly clear up the trouble.

Constipation

Sometimes, though infrequently, a bird may be suffering from constipation, in which case the signs of straining on defaecation will be apparent. Treatment is simple, consisting of the addition of a few drops of oil to the seed mixture. If this treatment fails, then sufficient epsom salts to cover the end of the handle of a teaspoon should be added to the water. Should this also fail, then it is possible that there is a blockage of the bowel, and tumour cannot be discounted. Usually, a case of simple constipation should clear up within two days at most. If it does not, then some other more serious cause must be suspected.

Tumour

Budgerigars, like all other forms of animal life, are subject to the development of tumours. These may manifest themselves in any part of the body, and the signs may not be immediately apparent. In cases of tumour, there will be none of the readily distinguishable signs of disease as with respiratory or alimentary diseases, and the situation will almost certainly arise at which the bird has been developing the tumour for some time before signs of it appear.

The breeder will have to decide for himself whether a bird suffering from a tumour should be kept, or painlessly destroyed. If, for example, the tumour is evident in the neck of the bird, then it will not be able to take food and will almost certainly be in pain. In such a case, there is no choice in the matter. On the other hand, as the tumour develops, the bird will lose weight, and if the tumour is in some part of the body which is unknown, perhaps the liver or kidney, this will be the only sign of anything amiss, until the tumour grows to large proportions. There are two types of tumour; the benign, which will simply grow at one place, and the malignant type, commonly called cancerous, which will spread throughout the body.

EYES

Budgerigars can contract eye diseases in the same manner as all animals. The probable cause of minor eye ailments, blepharitis, which is inflammation of the eyelid, or conjunctivitis, inflammation of the conjunctiva, is dirty perches; the birds causing the inflammation themselves when rubbing their beaks and heads in the dirt.

The primary treatment for both conditions in which inflammation will be apparent, is bathing with a weak solution of boracic crystals, but if the condition persists, veterinary advice should be sought and some form of antibiotic cream applied.

Cataracts

A cataract is an opaque curtain which descends over the eye and in Budgerigars, it is inoperable. A milky white film will be seen over the eye itself, and this will render the bird blind in that eye. It will not cause pain, and a bird which has a cataract on one eye may be kept, all other things being equal. If, however, the bird develops cataracts on both eyes, then it will be totally blind and should be destroyed.

PARASITES

We have referred several times to red mite, the most common parasite affecting Budgerigars, and although they are by no means as common as they once were, largely because of the efficiency of modern insecticides, the beginner should be aware of their existence and the methods of combatting them. There are several types: the red mite, the grey mite, sometimes referred to as the northern mite, depluming lice, which attack the feathers and cause them to fall out, and the scaly mite, to which we have already referred. These mites, with the exception of the one which causes scaly-face, live in minute crevices in the cages, emerging from their hiding places at night to feed from the bodies of the birds. If the bird room becomes heavily infested, the stock will certainly suffer, and breeding operations will be badly affected.

Treatment is by the use of one of the proprietory anti-mite sprays available from pet stores; the one which I have always found to be very effective in preventing these pests gaining a foothold is Johnson's Anti-Mite, though there are others, which I would not doubt are equally effective. Regular spraying of the bird room and the birds, perhaps once every month, will, in most cases, entirely prevent infestation.

FRACTURES

Stories abound of people setting broken wings, which can occur by accident, especially in a flight. The chances of such an operation succeeding are, however, extremely remote and should not be attempted by the breeder. If the bone protrudes through the skin, veterinary attention should be sought immediately. If the fracture is simple, the bird should be isolated in a small cage, preferably a show cage, over the front of which is hung a light cloth keeping the interior dim, but leaving enough light to enable the bird to see. The perch should be placed as close to the floor of the cage as possible and close by the water pot, thus ensuring that the bird is not forced to move any more than is absolutely necessary.

The bird should be kept like this for two weeks, following which it can then be placed in a single stock cage, again with the perch close to the bottom of the cage. After another two weeks the wing will have healed, and, assuming that the bird is able to fly, it may be placed back in the flight or in its larger stock cage. It is almost always the case with fractures of the wing, that the affected wing will be permanently damaged, and the wing carriage will be completely ruined.

Fracture of the Leg

The treatment of a fracture of the leg will depend upon the position of the break. If it is high on the thigh, the best treatment is as described above for fracture of the wing. If the break is on the lower leg, however, it may be possible to apply a splint. Two people will be needed to apply such a splint, one to hold the bird and the other to tie it.

The best method is to use a split crow quill, which will be found to be of the correct proportions. The quill should be cut to the required length, and then split along its length. A thin pad of material is placed around the leg and tied loosely with cotton. The split length of quill is then placed over the pad, and tied securely in place, the whole thing then being covered with a cotton wool pad. When the operation is completed, the bird should be left as previously described and should be kept as quiet as possible.

FRENCH MOULT

There is a condition which arises in Budgerigars which has troubled breeders for many years, known as French Moult. The reason for this condition causing problems is that although there are many theories concerning its cause, none has been proven to date. As we have already seen, the feathers of a Budgerigar are comprised almost solely of protein in one form or another, and at present, the theory on the causes of French Moult which I believe has most support, is that it is caused by protein deficiency in the diet.

The main signs of the condition are that in the young and developing chicks, the primary flights, those on the edge of the wing, and the secondary flights, those immediately adjoining, the tail feathers, and sometimes the smaller feathers will fall out, preventing the affected bird from being able to fly, and originating the term 'runners', usually used by fanciers to describe such birds. The condition may also manifest itself in the form of malformation of the feathers, which, instead of growing to their full length, will be shorter than normal, and may have curved quills. The feathers are also much softer than is normal and may have a distinctly deformed appearance.

Many theories have been propounded on the causes of this condition. For example, I met a fancier who was most definite that the correct treatment for French Moult was to feed the stock with soaked seed which had been treated with Australian honey. Certainly the breeder concerned had no French Moulting in his bird room, and had not had any problems for several breeding seasons. The same breeder was, however, extremely conscientious on the feeding of his stock, and supplied correct amounts of vitamins, proteins and so on, and it may well be that because of that, he had eliminated the condition from his stock.

There is a theory that a minute form of mite is responsible for the condition, and another which appears to indicate that there is some form of hereditary factor involved. Much research has been carried out into the causes of the disease by very eminent people, but at present, the precise causes are uncertain. My own opinion, and I stress that it is an opinion and not necessarily a fact, is that the protein deficiency theory is probably correct, knowing as we do, that the provision of protein is essential for growing feathers. It must surely follow that a deficiency of the substance will have a detrimental effect on that growth.

The breeder should also be aware that a stud which has never produced a runner may suddenly produce several in one breeding season, and for no apparent reason. If this happens, then in my view, the breeder should re-examine his entire feeding programme and increase the protein intake of the birds.

Because of the possibility of some hereditary factor being involved, Budgerigar breeders do not breed from birds which have suffered from French Moult, and such birds are disposed of to pet shops at the earliest opportunity, quite regardless of the fact that they may have, for example, outstanding head qualities. This is very much a case of being better safe than sorry, and I agree entirely with those sentiments.

GENERAL REMARKS

In treating diseases of Budgerigars, a large element of luck is needed. In many cases, for example in gastro intestinal disease, the bird will not respond to the first antibiotic which is given. As we have already noted, such diseases will quickly kill a bird, and if the organism causing the disease is resistant to the antibiotic, the outcome will in all probability be the death of the bird before the correct medicine can be identified. If a bird is found to be suffering from a disease which cannot be absolutely identified immediately, all one can do is to give whatever antibiotic happens to be quickly available, because speed is of the essence. Even a few hours delay can mean the difference between saving or losing a valuable bird.

It should also be remembered that post mortem examination may be of extreme importance in cases where the specific cause is unknown, in order to prevent the spread of the disease throughout the aviary, or to enable the breeder to be ready with the correct and effective treatment if any other bird should begin to show the same signs of disease.

Hospital Cage

In all Budgerigar diseases of a more serious nature than something of the order of simple diarrhoea, treatment consists in the first instance of isolation and warmth. In its simplest form, this can consist of placing the patient in a show cage, at an appropriate distance from a source of heat, e.g. an electric fire, or some similar appliance. A much more precise method is available, however, and its use is recommended. This device is known as a hospital cage, and its value in any bird room is very high indeed when it is needed. Hospital cages are available commercially, but are quite expensive considering their rather simple construction.

Basically, a hospital cage is not a cage at all, but a wooden box, with two compartments, one approximately one foot by one foot by one foot, the other around nine inches by one foot by one foot placed one on top of the other. The two compartments are separated by a wire mesh floor; the upper compartment has a glass front, and contains a thermometer and a single perch set close to the floor. The seed and water pots are placed within easy reach of the perch. In the sides of the upper compartment, and near the top, ventilation holes are placed. The lower compartment has a solid front, and contains two 60watt electric light bulbs, which have metal covers over the top. The bulbs are connected to the electricity supply in such a way that one or both may be switched on at any given time in order to regulate the temperature in the upper compartment. This should be controlled at 80 degrees Fahrenheit in the first instance, being gradually reduced as the bird becomes progressively better. In such conditions, it is important to change the drinking water frequently, as well any nourishing soft food containing egg which is being given.

INDEX

203

break in training, 124-5

Nest boxes, 87, 89
  desk type, 89
  drawer type, 89
  materials, 90, 92
  rectangular type, 89-90
Nest feather shows, 131
Night lights, 104
Noise, 56-7
  see also Bird rooms: avoidance of external distractions

Oils, 47-8
Open shows, 131
  information in press, 133
Outcrossing, 159-60
Painting
  bird rooms, 25-6
  breeding cages, 28-9
  carrying cases, 132
Parasites, *see* Pests and parasites
Perches, 29
  in breeding cages, 87
Pests and Parasites, 194-5
  mites, 57-8, 194
  vermin, 58
Phenotypes, 149
Planning permission, 10
Pneumonia, 190
Price of breeding stock, 62
Progeny testing, 156-7
Protein, 39, 41
Psittacosis, 191

Records
  breeding register, 114
  importance in colour production, 183
  of egg laying, 95, 97
  of matings, 92
  ring numbers, 106
Respiratory system diseases, 188-91
Ringing
  closed, 82
  technique, 106-7
  split celluloid, 107

204

Roof covering, 16

Temperature control
  by lining walls, 17
  thermostat, 20
Thrush, 189
Tonic seed, 51-2
Training
  break during moult, 124-5
  cages, 34, 36
  problems, 123-4
  units, 121, 123
Tuberculosis, avian, 190
Tumours, 194

Undershot beak, 109-10

Ventilation, 14-15, 16
Vermin, 58
Vitamin additives, 44-6, 52

Water, 48, 52
  pots, 31
Weaning, 111-112, 114
Wheat germ oil, 47
Wholemeal bread and milk, 50-1
  for chicks, 106
Windows
  external protection, 34
  positioning, 14-15

Yellow feather, 80